Bill Cosby

FAMILY FUNNY MAN

Bill Cosby

FAMILY FUNNY MAN

LARRY KETTELKAMP

Jonathan Evans

Wanderer Books
PUBLISHED BY SIMON & SCHUSTER, INC.,
NEW YORK

All rights reserved including the right of reproduction in whole
or in part in any form. Published by JULIAN MESSNER/
WANDERER BOOKS Divisions of Simon & Schuster, Inc.,
Simon & Schuster Building, Rockefeller Center, 1230 Avenue
of the Americas, New York, New York 10020. JULIAN
MESSNER, WANDERER and colophons are trademarks of
Simon & Schuster, Inc.

10 9 8 7 6 5 4 3 2 1

10 9 8 7 6 5 4 3 2   pbk

Manufactured in the United States of America

Design by Thomasina Webb

Library of Congress Cataloging-in-Publication Data

Kettelkamp, Larry.
  Bill Cosby: family funny man.

  Bibliography: p.
  Summary: Examines the life and career of the popular
entertainer, from his childhood to his success as a
comedian and actor.
    1. Cosby, Bill, 1937-   —Juvenile literature.
  2. Comedians—United States—Biography—Juvenile
literature. [1. Cosby, Bill, 1937-   . 2. Comedians.
  3. Entertainers. 4. Afro-Americans—Biography]
  I. Title.
  PN2287.C632K48 1986   792.7'028'0924 [B] [92]   86-23809
  ISBN 0-671-62382-6
  ISBN 0-671-64029-1 pbk

DEDICATION

To Gavin White, Jr., who generously shared experiences and offered personal encouragement with this project

"I have just finished the book. It is most enjoyable, and I'm positive it will be a success. In fact, I read it twice, and twice I had a lump in my throat. It's probably because I know the Cosbys and read your pages in 'living color.' Bill is a very good example of doing well in life in spite of the obstacles. As they say, 'when the going gets tough, the tough get going.' Bill is a self-starter for sure."

Doris White, Wildwood Crest,
New Jersey, 1986

CONTENTS

INTRODUCTION

Bill Cosby is one of today's most popular entertainment personalities. His reputation as a comedian and actor and his status as a family man and father figure to fans of all ages attest to the remarkable career of a remarkable man. The most visible of his current accomplishments is "The Cosby Show," the series in which he entertains and educates millions of viewers. The series is the number one comedy on television. But this is only the most recent in a long string of achievements.

When he started out in Philadelphia and New York as a stand-up comic, Bill developed appealing routines based on his own personal experiences in childhood, in school, in the navy, and among his family. A devoted father of five, Bill has managed to balance the demands of family and career in a way not often achieved by someone so consistently in the public eye.

Gifted as an athlete, Cosby excelled in a variety of sports including track and football. He attended college on an athletic scholarship and almost went into professional sports later on. His decision to become an entertainer put an end to his sports career and interrupted his plan to become a teacher. However, Bill eventually made a contribution to education by working on such television shows as "The Electric Company" and his own animated series, "Fat Albert and the Cosby Kids." The Fat Albert project later served as the basis for an advanced degree in education.

Bill Cosby has starred in both television and films as a dramatic actor. He has had his own TV variety shows and situation comedy series. He has put out well over a score of comedy and music albums. He is a businessman, producer, and author.

None of these goals has been easily reached, and there have been failures as well as successes. Born to a family of limited means following the Great Depression, Bill had to accept more responsibility early in life than is required of most youngsters. At one time a high school dropout, he nevertheless eventually went on to finish college. That he accepted challenges and turned them to his advantage is a tribute to Bill's persistence, a characteristic he has demonstrated throughout life.

Bill Cosby has received awards almost too numerous to count, including three Emmys and eight Grammys. In fact, he has so frequently been honored that he now refuses as many nominations as he accepts. Of his many achievements, perhaps two best symbolize Cosby and his philosophy. One is his doctorate in education from the University of Massachusetts. The other is his book, *Fatherhood*. Above all,

Bill Cosby's mother Anna and wife Camille, 1966.

Bill Cosby is an educator and a parent with a purpose
that shows clearly through everything he does.

The story of how Bill Cosby came to be the person we know so well today is told in the pages of this
book. It is an intriguing journey through time with
twists and turns, accidents, incidents, and anecdotes.
It is the story of a person with strong roots, relationships, and family ties, who has been both helped and
helper along the way. And the common thread through
it all is the humor of a man who sees the world through
laughing eyes. It is literally the story of Bill Cosby:
Family Funny Man.

1

FROM SCHOOL DROPOUT TO NAVY, SPORTS, AND COLLEGE

William Henry Cosby was born on July 12, 1937, in a black neighborhood in the section of North Philadelphia called Germantown. His parents, William and Anna, had moved north from Virginia during the Great Depression. William Henry was their first child, and he was born during those difficult times. William senior worked as a welder, and for a while the family got along rather decently. Two years after William Henry another boy, James, was born. Later on, two more boys, Russell and Robert, completed the family. Russell was five years younger than William, or Bill, as he was called. Robert was almost nine years younger.

During these early years, the Cosbys moved from their first place on Beechwood Street to an apartment on Steward Street. Bill remembers sleeping with his brother, James. He also remembers that the new apartment had no bathtub, only a portable metal tub, which could be filled with water that had been heated on the stove. Taking a bath was not a very enjoyable experience.

Bill's next younger brother, James, was often ill as a child. He tragically died of rheumatic fever at the age of six. To make things worse, Mr. Cosby had more and more difficulty holding a steady job, partly because he had a drinking problem; he was, in fact, an alcoholic. The income became erratic, and occasionally the family had to go on welfare. Mr. Cosby's solution to the problem was to join the navy as a ship's mess steward, or cook. Certainly this was a steady job, but it meant that he would be away a great deal, sometimes six or seven months at a time. As it turned out, the money he sent home was not always enough to support the family.

Bill's mother, Anna, began working as a maid, earning only about eight dollars a day, even when she could get steady work. This meant that the boys had to try to get odd jobs to help make ends meet. The family could not afford to stay in the Steward Street apartment, and so they moved into a unit in the Richard Allen Homes, a low-income housing development usually called "the projects" by everyone in the neighborhood.

While his mother was out of the house earning money, young Bill was left in charge of his brothers, Russell and Robert. Bill acted as older brother, makeshift father, and baby-sitter all rolled into one. It certainly was a large responsibility for a youngster, yet Bill mostly remembers the good times. His solution to the problems that came along was to develop a sense of humor. For example, he added food coloring to scrambled eggs or pancakes when cooking for the boys. Blue and green, their favorite colors, turned ordinary food into fun food. This playful outlook on life was to be expressed later in Bill's special brand of stage humor as a comedian. The events of his childhood also became the seeds for his now famous monologues about his brothers and other youngsters in the neighborhood.

Some of these childhood stories are now available on Bill Cosby's records. Although the situations are exaggerated, there is a ring of remembered truth about them that reminds many listeners of their own family problems. Bill jokes about trying to give his little brother Russell a bath in the toilet, perhaps a logical substitute for the missing bathtub in the mind of a mischievous youngster. He also jokes about discipline. According to Bill, the children called their father "the giant." In recalling physical punishment for misbehavior, Bill tells a story about Russell sitting at the table laughing, pointing at his father's face, and saying, "Daddy's got a funny face. Ha, ha, ha. Daddy's got a funny face." In Bill's version of the story, Russell gets smacked in the face, and his lips and eyeballs are knocked off and go rolling onto the floor. Thus a family problem becomes wildly funny through Bill's keen imagination.

Although William senior was not a harsh man and even had his own dry sense of humor, his drinking problem and his long absences took their toll on the family. Much later, when speaking of the word "father," Bill commented, "The word still spells disappointment to my brothers and me."

In the absence of a father, Anna Cosby became the chief supporter of the family. She found it difficult to discipline the children directly, and whenever one of them did something wrong, she would dissolve into tears. The reality of their family situation and the neighborhood in which they lived made it tempting for the Cosby boys to follow some of their peers into a life of vandalism and theft. Bill believes that his mother's extreme distress over any misbehavior acted as a deterrent to him as he grew up. He behaved himself because he did not want to let his mother down.

When he was around nine years old, young Bill began trying to earn money in his spare time to help support the family. One of his first jobs was shining shoes. He made a shoeshine box out of an orange crate and carried it downtown in search of clients. Within a few years, Bill was spending his summer vacations working in a grocery store. On weekdays he labored from six in the morning to six at night, and on Saturdays from six in the morning to nine at night. He arranged produce on the shelves and delivered groceries to customers. When school was in session, Bill got up early to sell fruit on Marshal Street before classes began. After school, he came home to keep an eye on his younger brothers.

SCHOOL DAYS IN PHILADELPHIA
Mrs. Cosby was a firm believer in the value of education. She insisted that her children attend school regularly and work to maintain high grades. Bill, who attended the Mary Channing Wister Elementary School, took to sports but not to academic work. Fortunately for Bill, during both the fifth and sixth grade

7

years he had a devoted teacher named Mary Forchic. Bill was in the class designated for youngsters who were "difficult to teach," which was taught by Mary. She had a great deal of patience and respect for her children. Bill remembers her taking them on trips downtown. She also made it a practice to visit the families of children in her classes. She would appear after dinner, usually with some sort of gift of food in hand, well aware of the needs of many of the families in her district. The Wister School was racially mixed, but Miss Forchic made no distinction between blacks and whites in her classroom. This was an important influence on the students in a world in which blacks were often treated as second-class citizens. She believed that education was the way to equality for all individuals. Bill was to grow up remembering the impact of Mary Forchic as a model teacher.

At home Bill encountered secondhand another educator who presented a realistic view of the relationships between whites and blacks. This was author Samuel Clemens, better known as Mark Twain. Some readers criticized him for portraying blacks as slaves and servants. Yet in Mark Twain's time those were the roles allotted to blacks, and so he was describing things as they were. But in Twain's books characters who were black or white, rich or poor, all existed together with no one being superior to anyone else. Indeed, his blacks and whites developed close friendships. Furthermore, Mark Twain was a humorist who poked fun at anyone of any race or social position, yet showed respect for all of them.

Anna Cosby often read Mark Twain's stories to

her children. One was *Pudd'nhead Wilson*, a tale about a bad-tempered boy whom nobody could control. Another was *Tom Sawyer*, the popular novel that included the scary story about the adventures of Tom and Becky Thatcher in a cave, a section that Bill Cosby remembered clearly years later. Mark Twain's humorous storytelling style made a strong impression on Bill, and by age eleven he had begun to amuse people with funny stories and anecdotes of his own.

At school Mary Forchic tried to channel this comic talent by putting him into some of the class plays. One such play was called *Back to the Simple Life*. Miss Forchic also let Bill tell funny stories at school assemblies. Bill, a popular student, became captain of the track and baseball teams at Wister and was elected class president one year.

Bill could not apply the same energy to his studies as he did to everything else, however, and his urge to play the jokester and wise guy often erupted during class, interrupting the lesson. His report cards were so bad that more than once he forged his mother's signature on them to avoid having to bring them home and disappoint her. One time Miss Forchic sent a note home with Bill's school report. She had written, "In this classroom, there is one comedian, and it is I. If you want to be one, grow up, get your own stage, and get paid for it." Little did Mary Forchic realize at the time that her stern advice would come true years later for her brash young student.

Although he grew up to be six feet tall, in grammar school Bill was so much shorter than the other boys that he earned the nickname "Shorty." The name stuck, and his friends used it even after he had shot up to full size. After he became a successful comedian and actor, Bill invited his old Philadelphia friends out to visit him in California, sometimes even paying for their trip. Some were so impressed by his success that they felt awkward at first. But Bill said he could tell when they finally felt comfortable, because then they would all call him Shorty again.

After Wister Elementary School, Bill attended Fitz-Simons Junior High (Simons is pronounced with a long "I"), where he continued to be more interested in sports than in classes, and where he became captain of the tumbling team. In grade school Bill had been in special classes for youngsters who were hard to teach. Nevertheless, in junior high he was classified as a gifted student on the basis of an IQ test. This qualified him to enter Central High School, a boys' school where academic work was stressed more than in the other schools in the area. Central also had more white students than black.

Once at Central, Bill had the opportunity to play football, but he broke his arm during the first week of practice. After he recovered, he went on to participate in sports, but he found the academic work much harder than it had been in junior high. He carried on his practice of spending too much time on sports and too little on study, and so he flunked several courses. He compensated by becoming a ham and a clown in class and frequently got into trouble.

The best thing for Bill happened when he transferred to Germantown High, where blacks and whites were about equally mixed and the academic standards were less demanding. At Germantown Bill became captain of the football and track teams, and as his size and strength increased, he began to show increasing promise as an athlete. His running ability helped him to excel in both sports, and he steadily developed as a high jumper. But at the same time he continued the pattern of poor study habits. It became so serious that he flunked the tenth grade. During the repeated year that followed, his sports achievements were outstanding. Once, after a football game, a college recruiter came up to Bill and said, "I want you to go to Penn State." The offer would have meant a chance for Bill to attend a top football college on an athletic scholarship. But as soon as the recruiter learned that it was the young star's second year in the tenth grade, he correctly assumed that Bill was a poor student. The recruiter threw up his hands and walked away. It was hard for the young Cosby to realize that lack of study had closed the door to an opportunity that might never come again.

Discouraged with school, Bill dropped out and began working at various full-time jobs. He became an apprentice in a shoemaker's shop. The job was so boring, however, that he amused himself by nailing high heels onto the men's shoes. After losing that job, he worked in a factory that manufactured automobile mufflers. Pay was low, the job was a dead end, and Bill's future as a young laboring man looked bleak.

NAVY SERVICE AND NAVY SPORTS

At this time, some of Bill's friends joined the air force in search of a career with better pay. Bill decided that being in the military might be a good idea, but he was determined to be different and so he joined the navy, just as his father had done when Bill was a child. At first, in the navy Bill had an opportunity to travel. Then he was stationed at the U.S. Naval Hospital in Bethesda, Maryland, where he was trained as a medical aide, working with ill and crippled sailors.

Along with his medical training, Bill joined the navy track squad. He began to excel at sprinting and the high jump, winning various track awards in competitions between the navy squad and those of other military services, universities, and colleges around the country. Bill improved his time in the 100-yard dash to 10.2 seconds, a very respectable showing. And at a national Amateur Athletic Union meet he achieved his all-time best in the high jump—6 feet 5 inches, a very good height in the era before the Fosbury Flop, when the jumper arches over the bar backward, was introduced.

During his years in the navy, Bill Cosby realized that it was not a career he wanted for a lifetime. The only way out seemed to be education. A few of his navy buddies were taking correspondence courses in various subjects. Bill followed suit by enrolling in a correspondence course that enabled him finally to get his high school equivalency diploma. This meant that Bill now could qualify for college entrance if there was only a way to get there. One possibility was to take advantage of his current track activities.

COLLEGE ON A SCHOLARSHIP

During the track meets, Bill came into contact with teams from various colleges. One invitational meet was

Cosby as a college student wearing his letter sweater; the T stands for Temple University.

held at Villanova University. Among the schools represented was Temple University, a private college in Philadelphia with a good reputation in intercollegiate sports. At the meet, Bill introduced himself to Gavin White, the Temple track coach. White had been impressed with Bill's performance in the high jump, and as it happened he needed a jumper who could pick up points in other events as well. Coach White looked at Bill and asked, "How high do you jump?" Without batting an eye, Bill answered, "Seven feet," to which Coach White countered, "Really? At Temple we accept only five-eighters."

The good-natured banter was the start of a comfortable relationship. The two men went on to discuss Bill's chances for further schooling and sports competition after his navy stint was completed. The upshot was that Gavin White recommended Bill to Ernie Casale, athletic director of the college, for a full athletic scholarship at Temple University.

And so at twenty-three, an age at which many college students have already completed undergraduate work, Bill entered Temple, where he majored in physical education and minored in psychology. As a freshman, Bill had the disadvantage of his minimal high school education, but the advantage of his experience in the navy and his physical maturity. The Temple scholarship covered his tuition and fees but not his living expenses. Bill worked at odd jobs and occasionally borrowed meal cards from friends as a means of skimping through. For the first time in his life he worked hard at his academic courses, aware that his scholarship depended on his maintaining the

Cosby excelled as a member of the track team at Temple University.
Here Cosby is about to release the discus.

necessary grade average. In spite of the time spent on sports, Bill achieved a B average during his first year. In the following summer he worked as a lifeguard.

As a member of the track squad Bill participated in a surprising variety of events, including the javelin throw, discus toss, shotput, high jump, long jump, and eventually even the 220-yard low hurdles. His skill levels were so high that in one track meet he placed first, second, or third in six different events.

During this period Bill acquired an unusual nickname. This came about when he was being trained for the 220-yard low hurdles—an event in which he had not competed before as a member of the Temple

15

Cosby preparing for the javelin toss.

squad. Before this, Bill had poked fun at the men running laps around the football stadium track. It happened that the pole vault pit was located beside the track close to the end of the 320-yard loop. Bill always kidded that a little man named Riggie hid behind the pole vault pit. As a runner came by reaching a point of exhaustion, Riggie would jump out and hit him in a leg muscle with a hammer. At least that is what it would feel like to the tired runner. Bill had borrowed the name Riggie from the words "rigor mortis," meaning the total paralysis of death.

When Bill joined the runners in the lap training, he experienced the same muscle fatigue. His teammates pinned the name Riggie on him, and the nickname stuck through his college days and later became the basis for one of his humorous stories.

In his story, Bill describes a relay in which he has to run the anchor lap. Just as his teammate completes the third lap, he drops the baton, retrieves it, and passes it to Bill. By this time, however, Bill is so frustrated that he bops his teammate on the head with it before making a belated start at his own lap. But as luck has it, Bill suffers leg cramps and falls down, unable to finish the race. In revenge, the Temple runner who had dropped the baton comes over to Bill, grabs it once more, and hits Bill over the head with it.

Actually, Bill never ran in relays at Temple. The story was neatly contrived out of his experiences with muscle cramps while training for the low hurdles. The relay setting simply makes the story more exciting.

Whether or not it was because Bill had a minor in psychology at Temple, he was a good judge of human personality. Part of athletics is the mentality of competition, and Bill went into everything psychologically as well as physically. A good example was a championship track meet of the Middle Atlantic Conference held at Rutgers University. Besides Rutgers, the meet included Lafayette, LaSalle, St. Joseph's, and Gettysburg. Temple was also participating, and as usual Bill Cosby was scheduled for several events.

Normally his best event was the high jump. However, Bill had not been reaching his potential lately; jumping only about six feet, not high enough to place well at the individual meets.

Just before the high jump competition, one of the Temple track men told Coach Gavin White that Cosby was going to win the championship that day. White thought the student was joking until he discovered that Bill was taking advantage of an unusual situation. One of the approach lanes to the high jump pit had been extended, and partway along it there was a bump in the grass. This was bothering some of the jumpers in practice. The day was very hot, and tents had been set up on the field so that participants could keep out of the sun. Bill was inside one of the tents talking in a very loud voice so that all outside could hear. He was complaining about the approach lane, saying, "That's really a terrible bump out there. There's no way anybody is going to jump over five-ten today."

Apparently Bill's "psych-out" had some effect. Amazingly, Cosby won the high jump with a leap of only six feet. None of the other competitors managed to move out of the five-foot numbers that day.

In spite of temporary slumps, the high jump continued to be one of Cosby's best overall events. Of course the coaching at Temple was very good. But in an unusual series of circumstances, the college Bill was now attending had prepared Bill for this event many years earlier. Bill had begun high jumping in junior high, and at that time the gym teacher at Fitz-Simons Junior High was Richard Lister, who himself had attended Temple University. Lister had been at

Temple when Gavin White was a student there, and both men had been on the track team. Lister's specialty was the high jump.

Bill never forgot the details of his early experience with Lister as his junior high teacher, and how much this early training contributed to his athletic skills and self-confidence. In fact many years after college, Cosby wrote about this in a book for young readers, *You Are Somebody Special,* compiled by Charles Shedd.

Bill recalls that in junior high he was only five feet three, still Shorty to some of his friends. Nevertheless he was strong enough to excel as a runner. Bill had never tried the high jump, but he was intrigued by a classmate named Sporty, who could high jump 4 feet 6 inches. To young Bill this looked like an amazing feat. He decided it would be fun to try it himself. So he ran toward the bar, stopped, and then jumped straight up, tucking in his legs. Of course, he landed on the bamboo crossbar and broke it—not a very good start to a high-jumping career.

Fortunately Richard Lister came to the rescue. Because of his college track experience, Lister had taught Sporty how to jump, and now he offered to teach young Bill the same technique. In those days the popular forms for high jumping were the Western Roll, in which the jumper stretched out horizontally and went over the bar sideways, and the Eastern Roll, in which the jumper kicked one leg up over the bar, rolled over, and then followed up by kicking his jumping leg over last.

In order to teach Bill the Eastern Roll, Mr. Lister

set the bar at only two feet, which was embarrassingly low. But Bill swallowed his pride and practiced a five-step approach, learning how to roll his body horizontally while lifting himself up and over. Lister's instruction took hold, and with continued practice Bill was soon able to match Sporty at 4 feet 6 inches.

To Bill, it now seemed impossible to go any higher, since the bar appeared almost at eye level. He failed each time the bar was raised. Nevertheless, Sporty managed to clear 4 feet 9 inches, and Bill was determined not to let his friend get ahead. He remembers that on the next try he switched to a totally positive frame of mind and lost his fear of the new height. He even imagined people clapping as he went over the bar. On the next try, he cleared the bar easily but knocked it off with his trailing leg. On the subsequent try, he finally cleared the new height cleanly. For Bill, this was an important discovery in self-confidence, one he was to carry into athletic competition later at the college level.

At Temple, Bill Cosby not only starred at track but also was a fine player on the football squad. He wanted to play halfback and receive passes, to take advantage of his speed and flexibility. But, because he was strong and weighed 187 pounds, Coach George Makis made him a fullback instead. This forced Bill to do power runs and to spend a lot of time on defense. He did well enough to attract the attention of a football scout for the New York Giants. There was talk of a tryout with this outstanding professional team.

However, a career in professional sports was not to come about. Although he was doing well in sports

Cosby demonstrating the Eastern Roll in the high jump, his
best event.

at Temple, another interest became even more important to Bill Cosby. Everywhere he went, he continued his hamming, joke-telling, and storytelling, as he had in high school. Bill showed he had a gift for imitating Sid Caesar and other well-known entertainers. At the drop of a suggestion, he would also imitate friends and faculty members. Some of these take-offs became elaborate routines. For example, Athletic Director Ernie Casale used to brief the football team for games that would be shown on local television. Bill developed an exaggerated imitation of Ernie Casale warning the team about looking good at all costs and being careful not to scratch themselves in the wrong place while the TV cameras were on them.

Gavin White laughingly remembers another Cosby imitation. In addition to being Bill's track coach at Temple, White also coached the freshman football squad the year Bill was a member. One time the Temple team was scheduled to play an exhibition game at Gettysburg College. It was a night game and the only available facility was at a high school. The playing field was poor, and the outside lighting was so dim that the Temple players would not be able to rely on their usual strong passing game. The pass receivers simply would not be able to see the ball. To make matters worse, Temple players had to get to the locker room by going through the opposing team's locker room first.

Coach White was so disturbed by the poor playing conditions that he gave his squad a blistering pregame pep talk calculated to help them overcome all obstacles. At the end of the session, the players bolted for the door to the field, only to find it locked. In spite of the embarrassment, the Temple football team went on to play an excellent ground game and won decisively.

After the game, they boarded the bus for the ride home. To enable the coach to talk to the players over the noise of the engine, the bus was equipped with a mike and loudspeaker. No sooner had the bus filled than Bill Cosby jumped to the microphone and began a high-powered imitation of the coach's pep talk. It was a hilarious moment enjoyed by all but soon forgotten by everyone but Cosby.

Many years later Bill did a guest comedy appearance on the "Tonight" show, one of his first with host Johnny Carson. Gavin White tuned in that night to watch the program. To his surprise, Cosby's monologue was about a disgruntled football coach shouting at his team before sending them to the field, only to find the locker room door locked. No one in the viewing audience reacted more strongly to the routine that night than Coach White, who was startled to hear almost the exact words Bill had used in his imitation years earlier on the bus. It was an example of Cosby's uncanny memory, a gift he has put to excellent use in his comic routines over the years.

Bill also retained lasting impressions of other experiences at Temple and of the support he got from his teachers and coaches there. Years later, he was to comment, "I am very, very proud of the university. I was very happy when it accepted me, and when I was there. I think some of the happiest moments were when I was on the track team with Gavin White."

During the summer following his sophomore year at Temple, Bill got a job for $5 a night, along with whatever tips he could earn, working in a Philadelphia café. The establishment actually consisted of two facilities in the same building. One was called The Cellar, and the other was called The Underground. Bill began working as a bartender in The Cellar telling jokes and making money on tips. He mimicked or borrowed material from popular comedians such as

Mort Sahl, who was known for his political wit; Jonathan Winters; and rising comedian Dick Gregory. There was no stage, so Bill sometimes sat on a chair placed on a table because there was no room to stand up. He even had to climb over the bar to get to the table. The customers seemed to like his imitations and stories, so the owner occasionally arranged for Bill to substitute for the house comedian in The Underground.

Bill began to take advantage of other opportunities to entertain, realizing that he had a talent for working before live audiences. At the time, Bill's cousin, Del Shields, hosted a Philadelphia radio show. He was the first black employed by the station. Del sometimes invited Bill to the studio to do the warm-up, telling jokes to the audience to get them in a relaxed and friendly mood before the program started. Bill's opportunities to do such stand-up comedy only occasionally earned him enough money to be worthwhile, but he could sense that if he worked at it, he might be able to make a living as an entertainer later on.

Bill started to look for work in New York City. He auditioned for some of the clubs and restaurants in Greenwich Village, a section of lower Manhattan where many entertainers and comics got their start. In the winter of 1962 he was hired for $60 a week at a well-known club called the Gaslight, which also featured folksingers. Of course, Bill also needed a place to stay in the city, and the owner of the facility was kind enough to let him use an extra room above the club and not to charge him rent. Bill continued his studies at Temple University during the day, and traveled to New York to work as an entertainer at night. He stayed on at the Gaslight during the summer months between semesters, and his salary was increased to $175 a week.

One comic who already was popular at the time was Lenny Bruce. Bill Cosby was interested in Bruce's style. Bruce used true events as the source of his humor, and he had a unique delivery. At first, Cosby based his style on that of several other comedians, doing imitations of them at times. And like black comedian Dick Gregory, Bill frequently told racial jokes. However, he soon decided that racial humor was not his style. He was more interested in human situations that applied to almost anyone in any family, regardless of race or social class. And so Cosby began to rely more on his own experiences from boyhood, family life, high school, college, and the navy. It took him quite a long time to tell a joke, and initially some of the people in the audience were disappointed, because they had expected something different. But Cosby found that if he took his time and kept the personal approach, people gradually came around to laughing at his special point of view.

According to Bill, a big part of the work of being a comic was getting people to accept him enough to listen to him. He once explained, "People have to like you if you're going to be a comic. After a cat establishes the fact that he's funny, forty percent of the pressure is eased up on him because, when he walks out, people already like him."

During Cosby's summer run at the Gaslight, the *New York Times* sent a critic to see the new comedian.

The published review was very favorable and included a photograph. The critic wrote, "Mr. Cosby writes his own material. Although his output thus far is limited, his viewpoint is fresh, slightly ironic, and his best quips are extremely funny." This was some of the first important publicity Bill had received, and the article in the *Times* helped introduce the rising young comedian to a wider audience.

Bill decided he could use professional help with his career. He began working with a manager named Roy Silver. Silver started to record Bill's routines. He and Bill would go over the tapes to check the audience reaction to the jokes and to see which material was most effective. They checked the timing and the pacing of the material. Listening only to the tapes, away from the live situation, they could objectively analyze the flow of the routines. Some were too long or too awkward, even though the laughs were there. Bill and Roy Silver worked together to tighten and improve the old routines and to develop new material. Using the trial-and-error method, they kept the routines that worked best and discarded the rest. It was during this time, working with Silver at the Gaslight, that Bill developed some of his best early routines, all with an intriguing personal touch. One was the now famous routine about God and Noah speaking together about the building of the ark. Other routines were about playing football and learning karate, both based on Cosby's own sports experiences.

At the end of the summer, Bill received a brief booking at the famous Gate of Horn in Chicago for $200 a week. He barely had time to finish there when he had to get back to college for football practice. Working as a stand-up comic is not the kind of job to keep one physically active. Bill had gained weight and had to buckle down to get in shape. Once again he applied himself to his courses at Temple in an effort to keep up his good grade average. But his interest in a career as a comedian had begun to compete with school, and Bill's grades fell during his junior year.

Later that fall, Bill accepted a comedy gig at Philadelphia's Town Hall for $250 a night. But on the Friday night he was to appear there, the Temple football team was scheduled to travel to Toledo, Ohio, where they would play on Saturday. Bill asked for permission to go to Toledo by himself after the Town Hall engagement. The university rule was that all team members would travel in a group, and the football coach was not willing to make an exception.

Choosing between his desire to finish college and become a physical education instructor and his ambition to make it as a professional comedian presented a hard set of choices for Bill. After all, he was attending college on a full athletic scholarship. However, finishing school meant keeping his grades up as well as putting the necessary time and energy into sports. Although he knew it would disappoint his mother, Bill dropped out of Temple in November of his junior year. At that time he made a promise to himself: if it was at all possible, later on he would finish school and become a teacher. It was a promise he was to keep, although in a way he could not imagine at the time.

2
FUNNY MAN MAKES GOOD

In the early days of his budding career as a comic, Bill Cosby continued to employ Roy Silver as his manager. Cosby's nightclub fee gradually crept up to $500 a week, and he appeared successfully in prominent spots around the United States and Canada. These included the Fifth Peg in Toronto, the Shoreham Hotel in Washington, D.C., and the hungry i in San Francisco. During this time, he periodically returned to the Gaslight in Greenwich Village, where by now he was a fixture. His appearances on the West Coast kept Bill in touch with what was going on in the entertainment industry. At Roy Silver's suggestion, Bill hired a press agent, who got him more newspaper and magazine publicity.

During those early years, he played a club in Washington, D.C., called The Shadows. A friend in the area decided to arrange a date for Bill with Camille Hanks, who had grown up in nearby Silver Spring, Maryland. She was from a well-to-do black family, and her father, a colonel in the army, worked as a research chemist at Walter Reed Army Hospital. Camille had been attending the University of Maryland as a psychology major. She was nineteen years old.

When her friend first brought up the possibility of a date with Bill, Camille turned it down. But the two eventually met when Bill showed up at her bowling class. Bill kidded around and teased Camille about how poor she was at bowling. She decided that Bill was an interesting person after all, certainly amusing and not the loud type she had expected. Camille visited The Shadows to see his act and was impressed with Bill's talent. The couple hit it off together and began dating. Bill says that the first time he saw Camille, he told himself he was going to marry her.

Much of the time they were courting, Bill was entertaining at a club in New York City called The Bitter End. After his act, he would go to bed late, get up early, and drive all the way to Maryland to see Camille. They would spend a short day together, and then Bill would hurriedly drive 200 miles back to New York for his act in the evening. In spite of the distance, the romance flourished, and Bill and Camille became serious about wanting to be together permanently.

ENGAGEMENT AND MARRIAGE

Only three months after he met Camille, Bill proposed marriage. At first her parents refused to acknowledge the engagement. They objected to Camille marrying an entertainer who, in spite of making six or seven hundred dollars a week, seemed to be an unsettled person, always traveling, working strange hours, and having no secure future.

But Bill and Camille persisted, and gradually Camille's parents realized that Bill was not going to give up. After a while, they came to like him, even though they had reservations about his career. So they finally gave their blessing to the engagement, and in January 1964 Bill Cosby and Camille Hanks were married in Olney, Maryland.

Meanwhile Bill pursued his entertainment career. During the previous summer a comedian named Allan Sherman was hired to sit in for Johnny Carson on "Tonight." Sherman had already made several successful albums on which he sang parodies of well-known tunes. One was a letter home from a camper complaining about the facilities. This particular routine became so popular that it is still imitated—most recently in a soap commercial on television. Sherman took advantage of his own popularity to invite other entertainers onto the show. Earlier, Bill Cosby had auditioned three times for "Tonight" and had been turned down every time. However, Sherman was interested in Cosby and asked him to come in for another audition. Bill almost refused, not wanting to waste his time once more. Finally he agreed to audition for Sherman on a one-to-one basis. Sherman was delighted and booked Cosby for the show that same night.

Bill barely had time to prepare for the taping, which took place at five-thirty that afternoon. When Bill came on camera, he did his routine about a karate expert who wants to demolish a rock with a sharp blow. The expert says, "I'm thinking through this rock; I'm thinking two feet past it." Bill acts out the motions as he continues describing the expert. "He raised his arm and it came down." Cosby pauses briefly. "Unfortunately the rock was thinking, 'No you won't either,' and it shattered his whole elbow. . . . Now he picks on Jell-O."

As Sherman expected, Bill was a great success on the show. And his appearance on "Tonight" made Bill Cosby suddenly known to several million viewers who had never seen his live club acts.

It is interesting that Bill's humorous references to Jell-O later led to his doing commercials for that product. In these he talks with children, who seem as fascinated with the bouncy qualities of Jell-O as Bill must have been himself as a child.

Cosby's success had attracted a lot of attention, and toward the end of 1963 Warner Brothers offered him a contract to record a comedy album. The material was taped during a performance at The Bitter End. The album was called *Bill Cosby Is a Very Funny Fellow . . . Right!* It was produced by Roy Silver and Allan Sherman. Sherman wrote the copy for the back of the album sleeve, saying, "I wish I could look at your face when you first hear this album. I wish I could be with you when you first discover Bill Cosby. I don't know who you are; all I know is that you are one of the millions of people who buy records and who made my life so crazy and wonderful during the last year. I want to return the favor. That's why I'm so proud and happy for the chance to introduce you to Bill Cosby."

Sales of the album began slowly, but gradually it worked its way up the charts to a respectable number 21. Later, the album earned Cosby a Grammy Award for Best Comedy Album of the Year. Warner Brothers followed through by offering Cosby a contract for a second album. The material was taped live at Mr. Kelly's in Chicago. It was titled *I Started Out as a Child*. Like the first record, it was produced by Roy Silver and Allan Sherman. It, too, won a Grammy, and it earned over a million dollars in sales. This was the first album to include the childhood anecdotes that were to become such a vital part of Cosby's routines over the years that followed.

Bill's success brought a change in his personal life. Bill and Camille moved to the West Coast where Bill frequently appeared at clubs such as the Crescendo in Los Angeles, the hungry i in San Francisco, and Harrah's in Lake Tahoe, Nevada. He became close friends with the owner of Harrah's and has continued to appear there often ever since. It was during 1964, the year of his marriage, that Bill Cosby had an unusual opportunity to shift his career in a new direction.

TELEVISION AND DRAMATIC ACTING

TV producer Sheldon Leonard was casting a new adventure series. Leonard had successfully produced such series as "The Dick Van Dyke Show" and "The Andy Griffith Show." A close associate of Leonard's was the writer and actor, Carl Reiner. Leonard had seen Cosby on television, and Reiner introduced him-

In the TV series "I Spy," Robert Culp and Bill Cosby play secret
agents who travel as a tennis pro and a tennis coach. Here they pose
as a not-so-serious tennis team.

self to Bill after watching him do a show at the Crescendo in L.A. To Cosby's surprise, Reiner not only
complimented him on his act but invited him to meet
Sheldon Leonard. The result was that Bill Cosby was
offered an acting role in a TV series. Bill was hesitant
about accepting a role that demanded serious acting
as well as incidental humor. He agreed to take a screen
test, and the film clip suggested that he would be able
to handle the dramatic role.

The series was called "I Spy." Well-known actor
Robert Culp had been hired to play the leading part

of Kelly Robinson, an American CIA agent, who traveled to trouble spots around the globe posing as a professional tennis player. Cosby was to play Alexander Scott, a Rhodes scholar and CIA spy who traveled as Kelly's tennis trainer.

The show would require the two to do a lot of running and chasing. Of course, Cosby was a natural athlete, not to mention a good tennis player. Culp also had been an athlete in school and, like Cosby, had excelled in track. But the dramatic acting was another story. Culp was a professional; Cosby was not. In spite of his decent showing in the screen test, Cosby was so nervous in his first filmed episode that he appeared stiff and amateurish. Some NBC executives thought he should be replaced.

Robert Culp insisted that Bill would do fine once the series really got under way. He tried to help Cosby relax by giving him cues and frequent suggestions on how to handle a scene or how to react to the camera. Bill was a willing student, grateful for the guidance. He wisely realized that without some help he might fail altogether.

Culp and Cosby became close friends off screen. This tended to show up on the series, making a genuine team out of what otherwise might have been an awkward relationship. Another plus in the series was that it was shot on location in exotic places around the globe.

One worry for the executives at NBC was the response to casting a black man to costar with a white man. Some feared that broadcast affiliates in the South might reject the program. Fortunately, however, only

Bill Cosby and Robert Culp on location.

a few refused to air the show, and it received a wide national distribution. "I Spy" drew audience ratings in the top twenty shows. At the end of the first season, both Cosby and Culp were nominated for the Emmy as Best Actor in a Dramatic Series. No one was more surprised than Cosby when his name was read as the winner at the award ceremony. He had expected Culp to win because of his screen experience. The show continued successfully for two more seasons, and each season Bill Cosby won the Emmy.

Some critics faulted the show for thrusting a black actor into a role more typical of an upper-class white person. It was the same kind of criticism Cosby had received for refusing to do racial humor and refusing to take the part of an activist in the sit-ins of the

1960s. However, other critics saw it as an important breakthrough in television for black actors. Speaking in defense of "I Spy," Robert Culp said, "Audiences see two guys, not Bob Culp, white, and Bill Cosby, Negro. We're two guys who don't know the difference between a colored and a white man. That's doing more good than a thousand marches. We're showing what it would be like if there had been no hate." However, Culp also once said of Bill Cosby, "When he came in to read for 'I Spy,' he was scared and angry." Clearly Cosby had deep feelings about the difficulty black actors had in gaining acceptance. But he preferred to make a statement simply by doing the best job possible with his TV opportunities. Apparently, the success of "I Spy" opened the way for more black actors to secure more varied roles in television drama. For example, a later adventure series called "Mission: Impossible" starred black actor Greg Morris with a team of white actors.

After "I Spy" brought him fame, Bill's record sales tripled and his fee for one week of club performances rose to more than $25,000. Bill and Camille bought a Spanish-style home in Los Angeles. It had thirty-one rooms, including a guest room for Bill's mother, Anna. Bill offered to buy his mother a house in California. When she said she wanted to stay in Philadelphia, Bill paid off her mortgage and remodeled and improved her house.

FAMILY AND FATHERHOOD

Camille was pregnant when Bill first began working on the "I Spy" series. In April 1965, their first child,

Cosby as a proud new father holds his firstborn child, daughter Erika, in 1966.

Erika Ranee, was born. At the time Bill was in Hong Kong filming the show on location. However, when the baby was four months old, Camille, Anna, and Erika flew to Japan to be with Bill. Bill was crazy about the new baby girl and took to fatherhood without hesitation. Camille spoke of his attitude, saying, "As a father he's a very gentle man. He's just crazy about the baby and so patient. He loves to bathe her and feed her and dress her. He's just a very loving father. As a husband he has the same qualities." It was evident that, having missed the regular presence of his own father as a child, Bill was not going to let the same thing happen in his own family.

Camille Cosby and daughter Erika participate in a celebrity fashion show.

In the fall of 1966, a second girl was born to the Cosbys. Her name was Erinn Chalene. This time Bill had carefully engineered his shooting schedule for "I Spy" so that he could be home when the baby was due. Even so, Erinn arrived early and Bill nearly missed the event because he was filming a show in Denver, Colorado.

Because of Bill's achievements in entertainment and television, he was fast becoming rich as well as famous. One of his fascinations was expensive automobiles, and he soon acquired a garage full of them. He purchased a Mercedes-Benz 300SL. Soon he sold it and bought a Cadillac Eldorado, then a maroon Ferrari, a classic 1937 Rolls-Royce, and a new Shelby sports car. There was never any lack of smart-looking cars in which to take a ride. Sometimes Bill would just take off on his own for a long spin on one of the open California roads.

Although the Cosbys' first California house was not overly elaborate by Hollywood standards, it had a swimming pool, a sauna, a pool room, and plenty of space for entertaining. The Cosbys tended to be a quiet, closely knit family, but they enjoyed having friends over, including the Culps. Bill and Bob had become very close during the time they worked on the TV series together, and Bill and Camille also liked Culp's wife, actress France Nuyen. Because of his interest in music, Bill also came to know a number of prominent jazz musicians such as trumpeter and composer Miles Davis and drummer Elvin Jones. Because of his interest in athletics, he became friends with Wilt Chamberlain and other professional basketball players. At times Bill would even invite people all the way from the East Coast, including old friends from his early days in Philadelphia.

Bill enjoyed his new success as a television personality. Even so, although "I Spy" had been very well received, the ratings eventually slipped. Part of this was due to competition from similar spy shows. After three seasons NBC canceled the series. By this time, however, Bill Cosby had proved himself as an actor as well as a comedian, and he had made plans to branch out in various business ventures. An important step was forming his own production company along with Bruce Campbell and Roy Silver. It was called the

Campbell Silver Cosby Corporation. Smaller production companies were set up to operate as extensions of the corporation. One was Jemmin Productions, which was to handle television projects, and another was a recording company called Tetragrammaton.

Bill and Roy Silver had produced the first successful comedy albums, and now Bill decided to put out some music albums. These were a mixture of serious jazz and musical parodies somewhat in the manner of Allan Sherman. Bill wrote and sang some of the tunes. The style of the albums was rhythm and blues. One was humorously titled *Silver Throat Sings,* and another one was called *Hooray for the Salvation Army Band.* One of Bill's songs, "Little Ole Man," caught on enough to make the disc jockey charts for a while. During this period Bill even once went so far as to get a booking for himself as a singer rather than as a comic. It was at a club in Los Angeles called Whisky à Go Go. There was no way Bill's singing was going to outdo his comedy, but he has continued to get involved in musical projects all his life.

Another sideline was an involvement in radio. Coca-Cola was the sponsor of a five-minute daily program in which Bill did parodies of radio shows that had been popular in the past. One of these programs was called "The Green Hornet." On Bill's comic version he named the main character the Brown Hornet.

TV SPECIALS

Even before "I Spy" was canceled, Bill Cosby undertook other television projects. There were three Bill Cosby specials, which aired three years in a row. All were produced by Bill's own company. These were one-hour programs built solidly around Bill's special humor. The first one showed some film of Cosby visiting the Germantown neighborhood in Philadelphia where he had grown up. People gathered in the streets, and Cosby signed autographs for the neighborhood children. This was used as background for Bill's monologue about playing football in the streets and using the parked cars for defensive screens. Except for the Philadelphia scene, no one but Bill appeared on the show. He had decided to do the whole hour solo.

Some critics thought that this was a lopsided format for a TV special. Others praised him for keeping it simple and relying on his own strengths. In the two specials that followed, Bill did add more variety to the shows. He included dancers and singer Roberta Flack, who had become well known for her hit recording, "Killing Me Softly with His Song."

During the 1960s, much attention focused on the many demonstrations against racial prejudice. Many celebrities participated in these civil rights events, even risking arrest. Although Bill Cosby was not an activist, there was one event in which he became involved. On April 4, 1968, black minister and civil rights leader Martin Luther King, Jr., was shot and killed. On the day of the assassination Bill was playing in Kansas. The news shocked him. Bill started his last show of the night, thinking maybe it was best to follow the old rule: "The show must go on." But it was impossible for him to continue. The show was cut short.

Later there was a march in Memphis, Tennessee, in honor of Dr. King. Bill Cosby participated in the march along with his friend, Robert Culp. Many famous entertainers and politicians were there, walking side by side with people from across the country who came to Memphis for the march. It was an event Cosby was to remember well over the years that followed.

RETURN TO SERIES TELEVISION

Because "I Spy" had run for three years, it was natural that Bill Cosby soon would be considered for another television series. Bill created the concept for a new show for NBC. He was to be its executive producer, working closely with producer Marvin Miller. Bill wanted to play a physical education teacher. At first NBC executives resisted the idea. They had thought the role of a detective might be a good follow-up to "I Spy." But Bill persisted, and the idea for an educational setting won out. It was to be called "The Bill Cosby Show." Bill would play Chet Kincaid, and the setting would be Richard Allen Holmes High. The name was a reminder of the Richard Allen projects where Bill had grown up in Philadelphia.

While the show was to have humor, the plan was to create a realistic situation in which Chet would demonstrate both strengths and weaknesses. Chet would be helpful to his students. He also would get angry, make mistakes, and sometimes get carried away with his own ego. The humor was planned to come out of the human situations, instead of being contrived. Part of Bill's concept was to keep the show

low-key and casual, like the pacing of his own monologues.

Cosby thought that the show should have some
real educational values built in. He invited teachers to
check the script and the classroom details to make
certain everything was accurate. Some of the episodes
used actual lessons on politics, history, or ecology.
Sometimes the educational point was made through
failure rather than success. For instance, in one episode Chet and a guest star failed to save the trees on
a property where a building was scheduled to go up.
In another episode Chet tried to teach good sportsmanship, but he himself turned out to be a poor sport.

When the show first aired, some reviewers
thought that it had missed the track. They com-
plained that it was too slow-moving with too little plot
and not enough laughs. In spite of whatever faults it
had, it still rated number one against the other new
shows. Although it had slipped somewhat by the end
of the season, it still wound up at number eleven.
Seemingly many viewers liked watching Cosby, and
they apparently enjoyed the school setting. After all,
what could look more natural than Bill Cosby, a former athlete and physical education student, actually
teaching physical education?

"The Bill Cosby Show" was renewed for a second
season. But during the winter the ratings slipped further, and so the series was canceled after two seasons.
Nevertheless, it gave Bill Cosby a chance to try out
some of his own ideas for a show. It was the start of
a philosophy and format that was to become much
more successful later on.

3
FILMMAKER AND TEACHER

Cosby's roles on TV led to opportunities in films. Bill joined forces with Marvin Miller, who had produced "The Bill Cosby Show," in developing a motion picture set in the West. *Man and Boy* was a family picture that dealt with the problems of a family of black pioneers.

In *Man and Boy*, the family's only horse is stolen. Father and son trek about the country trying to find and recover the animal. The film portrays the typical problems of a black family confronting prejudice in addition to the hardships of life in the West.

Cosby and Miller had trouble getting financial backing for the picture. When Bill hesitated, his wife Camille urged him to go forward with the idea. And so Cosby and Miller started the film without any salary for themselves. Finally a backer agreed to put up money, and the shooting was finished. Cosby received praise for doing a good job of acting. The movie was barely strong enough at the box office, however, to pay back the production costs—around $800,000.

After *Man and Boy* came a second film opportunity. Bill Cosby and Robert Culp had seen a movie script about two down-and-out detectives trying to make a go of things in Los Angeles. The two actors felt that they could capitalize on their experience in "I Spy" and work as a team in the detective film. The Hollywood studio that held the rights to the story did not agree. So once again Bill embarked on his own venture. He and Culp purchased production rights to the script and found an investor to put up money for the project. At least with this film there would be an adequate budget from the start.

In the story, the two L.A. detectives, Hickey and Boggs, are down on their luck. Each has a broken marriage, and they don't have even enough money to rent an office. Robert Culp described the detectives' plight to a reporter in this way: "On a routine missing persons assignment, they stumble over several dead bodies. There is a fantastic amount of money involved, which they know nothing about. They can't find anybody, they don't know who anybody is, or what it's all about." The detectives tangle with mobsters and the police and wind up in gunfights and chases all over the city.

Although *Hickey and Boggs* had plenty of action and excellent photography, the critics thought the plot was too confusing and the detectives too serious. Apparently moviegoers agreed. A good acting job by Cosby and Culp was not enough to make up for the weaknesses of the film. It was not a success at the box office.

Bill Cosby and Robert Culp in a promotion shot for detective film, *Hickey and Boggs*.

During the course of his TV and acting projects Bill had become friends with the Oscar-winning black actor, Sidney Poitier. Poitier's popularity in movies had brought him enough money so that, like Cosby, he had begun producing his own films. Poitier was planning a film to be called *Uptown Saturday Night*. He was to be producer and director as well as actor. Several prominent black actors and entertainers had agreed to be in the movie. They included Richard Pryor, Flip Wilson, and singer Harry Belafonte. Poitier asked Bill Cosby to play one of the lead parts; Poitier himself would play the other.

The story revolves around Cosby and Poitier, two blue-collar workers who are gambling in a night spot. A gang of hoodlums breaks in to rob the establishment. Cosby loses his winnings, and Poitier loses a winning lottery ticket worth $50,000. In a way the film was similar to *Hickey and Boggs*. But the Poitier movie was full of crazy situations and laughs. The two stars, trying to recover their valuables, get a sermon from Flip Wilson and an introduction to Richard Pryor, who plays a detective who is too frightened to be effective. They are threatened by rival gang leaders, one of them played by Belafonte doing an imitation of Marlon Brando in *The Godfather*. They get cheated, chased, and beaten up, but they get back the money and the lottery ticket in the end.

Uptown Saturday Night was released in 1974. It quickly became a hit. Sidney Poitier immediately decided to produce another comedy adventure film as a sequel. It was to be called *Let's Do It Again*. In it Poitier and Cosby team up once more. The two are sup-

In *Let's Do It Again*, Cosby and Poitier are involved with the power of money for good and evil.

posed to help their lodge raise money for a day-care center. They decide to bet some of the lodge money on boxing matches to make more money. One of the fighters they promote is played by the young black comedian Jimmie Walker, who appeared on the TV series "Good Times." In the film, Poitier and Cosby work out a system of hypnotizing Walker so that he becomes a fantastic puncher, able to take on the champ, played by real-life former heavyweight champion George Foreman. The mob wants part of the fight winnings, and of course the lodge buddies find themselves in deep trouble. But just as in *Uptown Saturday Night*, they win out in the end and recover all of the money for the lodge. Again the Poitier-Cosby combination brought success. Reviews of *Let's Do It Again* were excellent, and the film broke records at the box office.

The two Poitier movies were followed by one produced by 20th Century Fox. It was called *Mother, Jugs, & Speed*. In it Bill Cosby plays an ambulance driver nicknamed Mother Tucker. Raquel Welch, a top actress, is also a member of the ambulance team. Another crew member is Larry Hagman, who later became famous as the conniving J.R. on "Dallas." The story is about an ambulance company trying to make a quick profit by grabbing up everyone at the scene of a disaster. Cosby was praised by movie critics for turning in a strong performance, but the film was panned for having too much sick humor about death and dying. Still, the response to the film was enough for it to be developed into a TV series. But the popularity Bill Cosby and Raquel Welch brought to the movie was missing in the TV series, in which other actors played the roles, and the series was soon canceled.

Bill Cosby played in several more motion pictures in the next few years. One was a third film with Sidney Poitier called *A Piece of the Action*. As with the two earlier Poitier films, the actors are a team. But this time there is a new twist as they enact the parts of cat burglars who seem to be good guys at heart. They only rob people who take advantage of the poor. The two burglars wind up going straight, and they

In *A Piece of the Action*, Bill Cosby and Sidney Poitier play two men who recover stolen gambling money for a good cause.

help youngsters in the neighborhood to straighten out and find jobs. The film was a mixture of drama, education, and humor. Though the idea was clever, the film was not as successful as the earlier ones starring Cosby and Poitier.

Another movie in which Cosby had a small part appeared in 1978. A play by Neil Simon, *California Suite*, was made into a movie. The stars included Bill Cosby, Richard Pryor, Jane Fonda, Michael Caine,

Walter Matthau, Maggie Smith, and Elaine May. The play traces four stories, two of them serious and two of them comic. Each story tells about visitors to California who stay in the same hotel suite at different times. The story is clever and the acting good. One of the best scenes is a fight after a doubles tennis match in which Cosby, Pryor, and their wives get hit with balls and rackets. Ironically, both comedians play medical doctors who wind up in bandages and casts. While Cosby was funny, the movie was not as much of a success as the play had been.

Bill Cosby made one more venture into movies in a film produced by the Walt Disney Studios, titled *The Devil and Max Devlin*. In it Bill costars with Elliott Gould, another actor who can combine comedy and straight acting. Gould plays a conniving landlord whose main pleasure is evicting tenants for no good reason. Finally the wicked man meets justice by being run over by a truck. He dies and finds himself in hell. There he comes face to face with Barney Satan, the character played by Cosby. Barney is even more evil than the landlord. He promises that Gould can return to life if he will search for the souls of three innocent children and bring them to Barney.

During the adventure, the landlord tries to double-cross his master, and Barney appears as the devil himself to take revenge on his wayward servant. Although the idea for the movie is ingenious, the plot is bogged down by the time Gould spends going after the children. The devil does not appear very often, so Cosby could not make a lot out of his role.

The Cosby family had moved to Hollywood in

1965 when Bill started work on "I Spy," and they lived there until 1971. A third child, their only son, was born to Camille and Bill in 1969. They named him Ennis William. During these California years, Bill spent as much time as possible with Camille and his young family. There were long stretches when Bill would be shooting for TV or films, but he would rush home to spend whatever time he had available. Even though Bill was a Hollywood star, the Cosby family was a traditional one.

DR. WILLIAM COSBY

In 1971 Bill decided to make an important change in his life. It was something he had been thinking about for some time. He had dropped out of Temple University to go into entertainment. His ambition at Temple had been to complete his education and become a teacher. In spite of all his other achievements, he still held that ambition. If he really was going to carry the intention through, however, he would have to go back to school and earn not only a master's degree but probably a doctorate as well. But how could he accomplish this when he had not completed college?

The answer came partly by accident. Like other comedians, Bill sometimes worked the college circuit, appearing at universities around the country where his humor was particularly popular. One of these schools was the University of Massachusetts at Amherst. Amherst seemed like a good place for Bill to pursue his studies. Later he was recruited by the school to take part in a project called the Special Program for Mature People.

The idea was to support people in the professions and politics in attaining advanced degrees with study programs tailored to their individual needs. The opportunity seemed ready-made for Cosby, and he agreed to join the program. Contact was made with Temple University. Officials there agreed to allow Bill credit for practical experience in education and courses he might take at the University of Massachusetts. In this way Bill could receive a bachelor's degree from Temple. It was not in physical education, however, but in communications. This was the same specialty within education that he would emphasize at the University of Massachusetts.

The plan also meant a change for the family and a move from the West Coast to Amherst so Bill could be near the college. The Cosbys chose a farmhouse just outside the university town in central Massachusetts. It was a dramatic change not only in location but also in life-style.

The 135-year-old house was located in a rural area on 286 acres of land. It had been built in colonial times and needed refurbishment. The work was done by a specialist in the restoration of colonial buildings, and it became a warm and comfortable home.

Inside the house were sixteen rooms and five working fireplaces. Outside were tennis courts, barns, and fruit trees. One of the barns was remodeled into an office for Bill. The other one became a special project. Many years earlier, Bill had promised himself that someday he would find a way to provide for his mother and repay her for all the sacrifices she had made when he and his brothers were growing up. And so the sec-

Bill Cosby with his wife Camille and mother Anna.

ond barn was converted into a home for his mother, Anna—a permanent and private place for her to live near Bill and his own family.

In Massachusetts two more children came along to complete the Cosby clan. In April 1973, another daughter was born. She was named Ensa Camille, taking her middle name from her mother. In 1975 the last child, also a daughter, was born. She was named Evin Harrah. Her middle name honored William Fisk Harrah, the owner of Harrah's resort in Lake Tahoe, Nevada, and Harrah's Marina Hotel in Atlantic City. The name was a gesture of friendship to the man who had become a close family friend over the years that Bill had played at the famous Nevada vacation spot.

All five of the Cosby children were given first names starting with the letter "E." When Bill was asked why this was so, he said that the "E" stood for excellence.

Amherst was a good location for the family of a famous person. The community was somewhat isolated by the surrounding hills and farmland. The Cosby children attended schools in the area and were readily accepted into the community. Nevertheless, sight-seers occasionally found the Cosby farmhouse, and a few would boldly drive right onto the property for a glimpse of the well-known star or his family. The No Trespassing signs seemed to have no effect, and so a special sign was placed at the driveway gate of the split-rail fence. It read, "If you are not invited, do not pass through these gates."

TELEVISION TEACHER

The graduate work at the University of Massachusetts was designed to take advantage of Cosby's experience in educational TV. Earlier he had worked regularly on the PBS series, "The Electric Company," produced by the Children's Television Workshop. This had grown out of the successful "Sesame Street," on which Bill also sometimes appeared. "Sesame Street" was a fresh and off-beat way to get very young children interested in learning through music, humor, lessons with an entertaining twist, and appealing characters like Big Bird.

"The Electric Company" was planned to go a step further and to actually teach children to read. The program introduced them to syllables and phonetic sounds with playful games and zany rhymes. Because

Cosby worked as a regular on public television for the Children's
Television Workshop. Here he appears on "Sesame Street."

it was produced for educational TV, the series had a
limited budget. Much of the money was used for research on teaching techniques that could be used on
the TV segments. But it was an exciting experimental
show, and Bill Cosby was happy to be involved, working for low pay and long hours compared with the gigs
as an entertainer to which he was accustomed. Cosby
became a teacher on "The Electric Company," using
his storytelling ability and his natural way with children to enhance the program. He was locked into the
format of the show, acting out his part for an unseen
Saturday morning audience of youngsters across the
nation. But Bill believed in the philosophy of the series and stayed with the show for two full seasons.

Along with his work on "Sesame Street" and "The
Electric Company," Bill came up with an educational

Cosby teaches reading on "The Electric Company."

TV project all his own. In many of his earlier monologues and recordings, he had told exaggerated stories
about his childhood friends. One character Bill used
was Fat Albert, a boy who weighed about "two thousand pounds." Everything shook when he walked
through the neighborhood. Bill decided to use his own
production company to create an animated cartoon
series based on the antics of Fat Albert and his friends.
All the characters were black, and they included
Dumb Donald, Old Weird Harold—who was about six
feet nine inches tall, just the opposite of Fat Albert—
Crying Charlie, and Rudy the Rich.

All of the animated characters were exaggerated
stereotypes. Fat Albert was the neighborhood bully
because of his weight. Dumb Donald had his mind off
in a cloud somewhere and became the victim of various pranks. Crying Charlie whined, and Rudy the
Rich owned everything that none of the other youngsters could afford. It was a slice of life turned into a
cartoon, and it was also educational. Every show
taught a lesson about good behavior, staying in school,
or learning to take responsibility. To reinforce the lessons, Bill hired a group of educational consultants, all
chosen by Gordon Berry, an assistant dean at UCLA
in California. Berry selected experts in everything from
child development and psychiatry to sociology and
communications. The experts read the scripts and
commented on the content of the series, which helped
to increase its educational impact.

Bill Cosby put the whole show together, doing
virtually everything but the cartoon animation. He introduced the show and closed it. Frequently he would

Cosby playfully sits down at Stevie Wonder's synthesizer during a break between scenes of NBC's "Motown Returns to the Apollo."

interrupt the animation to explain some point he wanted to get across. He also did the voices for some of the cartoon characters, just as he had done them in his monologues. This required trips to the studio to read and record parts of the script. Once when Ennis was young, Bill thought his son would enjoy going along with him. Ennis watched the show regularly at home. When he got to the studio, the boy was stunned to find out that Bill himself provided voices for Fat Albert and a few other characters. Afterward he said to his father with awe in his voice, "Dad, you mean *you're* Fat Albert?"

Bill began producing the program while he was still working in California. He called it "Fat Albert and the Cosby Kids," and it first aired as a special on CBS at the start of the fall school season in 1971. Reactions were good, and so the following year CBS picked it up as part of its regular Saturday children's programming, scheduled to be shown at lunchtime. The series did well in the ratings and ran for several seasons. While it was on the air, the show won many awards for its educational values.

For his degree work at the University of Massachusetts, Bill Cosby concentrated on using the Fat Albert material as a teaching tool. He produced student workbooks and teachers' guides so that schools could use the episodes of "Fat Albert" for classroom instruction. Eventually Cosby wrote two books based on Fat Albert: *The Wit and Wisdom of Fat Albert* and *Fat Albert's Survival Kit*. A comedy album called *Fat Albert* was released by MCA in 1973. Some time later, three videocassettes of the syndicated Fat Albert cartoons were made available by Thorn EMI Video.

The Fat Albert series also formed the basis for Cosby's doctorate in urban education. He turned in a lengthy thesis with an enormously long title: "An Integration of the Visual Media via 'Fat Albert and the Cosby Kids' into the Elementary School Curriculum as a Teaching Aid and Vehicle to Achieve Increased Learning." Another way of saying this might be, "How Teachers Can Use 'Fat Albert' in the Grade School Classroom." In his thesis, Cosby discussed the problems minorities face within the educational system and the elements of the show that could be used in an actual classroom.

Cosby and Bob Keeshan, TV's Captain Kangaroo, team up to produce a reading series called "Picture Pages." The series appeared as a regular feature on "Captain Kangaroo."

There were other educational ventures. Through PBS television, Bill had met Bob Keeshan, known to millions of youngsters all over the country as Captain Kangaroo. With the cooperation of the *Weekly Reader*, Cosby and Keeshan teamed up to produce "Picture Pages." This was a series of five-minute video programs aimed at teaching reading to preschoolers. "Picture Pages" appeared as a featured segment of "Captain Kangaroo" from 1980 to 1982, and comic books were sold for both home and school use.

Bill Cosby also was concerned about the problem of drug use among young people. With the support of CBS, Bill participated in a Saturday morning special focused on the topic. To point up the realities, three guests were asked to help with the program: a policeman familiar with neighborhood drug crime, a priest who operated a shelter for addicts, and an author who was an expert on drugs. Later Bill developed a record album for MCA in which he sings and talks in straight terms about the drug problem. The record is called *Bill Cosby Talks to Kids about Drugs.*

During childhood Bill had learned the hard way what alcohol abuse could do to his own father, and he was determined to avoid substance abuse himself. Once he discussed the drug question with a writer, and his comments were later quoted in the *Ladies' Home Journal:* "Every one of our children can testify that I told them, 'There will be no drugs!' I also let them know that I recognize the signs of drug and alcohol abuse, and so does their mother. And then, after all the love and education we give—and the warning that there would be some heads cracked—after all that, I think it's sometimes just luck."

After almost seven years of intermittent work, Cosby turned in his dissertation at the University of Massachusetts and appeared for an oral presentation before members of the faculty. He showed segments of the Fat Albert series and answered questions about his project. With these requirements for his doctorate completed, Bill Cosby appeared on the Amherst campus on May 19, 1977, in a black cap and gown to receive his degree from Chancellor Randolph Brom-

In May 1977, Bill Cosby becomes Dr. William Cosby as he receives his diploma in urban education at the University of Massachusetts in Amherst.

ery. Friends and family were at the ceremony, including Bill's mother, Anna, who was perhaps the proudest of all at her son's achievement. Newspapers covering the event noted that Bill had received an appointment to teach at Amherst. He was to be an adjunct professor in the media program and a faculty member for two years.

Cosby did not actually teach at Amherst, however. Although the school was praised by many people for its special degree programs, there were some who criticized the Department of Education at the University of Massachusetts for catering to celebrities and making it too easy for students to get a doctoral degree. People in the special program often were not required to spend time regularly on campus taking courses. One professor in communications, who objected to the practice, resigned from the university and wrote a book about the lack of standards in American education.

Whatever the criticisms, Bill Cosby's degree was not an honorary one. He had completed a program at a highly ranked university. He had fulfilled the degree requirements set for him, and he had done so using his own inventive teaching materials. From that point on, entertainer Bill Cosby could be called Dr. Cosby.

Over the years that he pursued his advanced degrees, Bill Cosby continued to work as an entertainer. CBS had carried his successful Fat Albert series, and in the fall of 1971, it presented a children's special, an animated version of the classic, *Aesop's Fables*. Bill played Aesop, the storyteller, in front of a live audience of children, who seemed to love the program.

Because of his accomplishments at CBS, Bill was given the chance to do a variety series called "The New Bill Cosby Show." It was to be produced by George Schlatter, who had produced "Rowan and Martin's Laugh-In," a wild 1960s show consisting of

Bill Cosby portrays the famous storyteller in the 1974 CBS production, *Aesop's Fables.*

skits which set a new style for TV comedy. Unlike Cosby's previous shows, this one was to include a variety of guest performers. Bill was to lead off each segment with one of his monologues. The rest of the show would be given over to routines and skits with the guest stars.

Harry Belafonte and Sidney Poitier were on the first show of the new series which premiered in 1972. Many other well-known stars appeared on later shows. They included Robert Culp, comics Lily Tomlin and Foster Brooks, and singers Roberta Flack and Diahann Carroll. The show came on at 10:00 P.M. Monday. This was perhaps too late for a family-type variety program. The show was lively, but the guest spots were not consistently interesting. Ratings were never high, and they fell even lower during the winter. Although the show ran for a full season, it was not renewed the following year.

After the mediocre reaction to "The New Bill Cosby Show," Bill did not become involved in another series until four years later. This time ABC kept making offers until Bill finally decided to try once again. The ABC show would air on Sunday at 7:00 P.M. It would be competing with "The Wonderful World of Disney," but otherwise it was a good hour for a family variety show. Part of the plan was for Bill to invite a youngster from the audience to be interviewed on camera during each show. ABC was counting on Bill's skill with children and children's humor to help attract an audience. The show was named "Cos," picking up a nickname that had become well known to Cosby fans over the years.

As on his previous variety shows, Cos would do monologues, and again a series of guest stars would make appearances. Once the show began to air, however, it seemed that a mistake had been made in trying to appeal to such a wide audience. The result was that the program was confusing. Critics said it was boring, cute, or inconsistent. Before the show started, Cosby had commented to a reporter philosophically on his experience in television saying, "My first series, 'I Spy,' ran three years. 'The Bill Cosby Show' lasted two years. My first variety show lasted one year. And this

Cosby first developed his ease with a live audience as a
stand-up comic.

show? If I'm lucky it will run thirteen weeks." In fact
the show did not do even that well and was canceled
after only seven weeks. Not even Cosby could be successful on television all the time.

NEW COMEDY ALBUMS

Along with his work in films, Bill Cosby continued to put out comedy albums. From time to time, his night-club shows were recorded. Even though he liked to repeat favorite monologues, he developed a great deal of new material as well, and eventually most of this showed up on records.

Cosby's audience for his records was very wide. Even in nightclubs where many comedians use "blue" material—four-letter words or jokes about sex—Bill usually stuck to material that appealed to children as well as adults. His topics were simply funny; slices of life with a comic twist in the telling. And so his records became favorites with people of all ages. It seems everybody could understand and appreciate Bill Cosby. It was not necessary that any of the recordings be immediate smash hits, although a few did start off with strong sales. For the most part, the albums just kept steadily selling and selling. Every time Bill appeared in a TV special or series or made a popular movie, he would gain fans, some of whom would begin to collect his recordings.

Bill's first two comedy albums, *Bill Cosby Is a Very Funny Fellow . . . Right!* and *I Started Out as a Child*, had been released by Warner Brothers and had done very well. Warners was so confident of Bill Cosby's appeal that over a period of years the company released six more of his albums, making a total of eight under one label.

Bill's third album was entitled *Why Is There Air?* It was recorded at the Flamingo Hotel in Las Vegas. It contained routines on football, a toothache, and driving in San Francisco in an automobile that cost $75. One of the car's faults was that it turned sideways on downhill streets. Perhaps some of the best material on the album is in the routine about kindergarten and first grade, in which Bill complains about everything from paper that was too rough to write on to the inedible schoolroom snacks.

Bill's next two comedy albums were recorded live at Harrah's in Lake Tahoe. The first of these is called *Wonderfulness*. It is indeed a wonderful collection of anecdotes about childhood. There are vivid and side-splitting descriptions of hospitals and playgrounds. One long routine recalls childhood fears triggered by radio horror programs. For instance, Bill describes how he put Jell-O all over the floor to trip up a monster called "The Chicken Heart." And he talks about other childhood problems such as what to do with the lumps in cream of wheat.

The other album recorded at Harrah's is called *Revenge*. More childhood horrors appear, such as a chilling account of how Bill and his friends become petrified while watching a spooky film at a movie theater, and then they have to walk home over the scary Ninth Street Bridge.

Revenge is the album in which Fat Albert is introduced as a boy who weighs 2,000 pounds. The gang plays a game called Buck, Buck, in which everybody piles on top of one person. The vision of having Fat Albert land on top of them strikes fear into the rest of the gang. The album title, *Revenge*, is taken from the routine about a snowball. During the winter Bill gets hit in the face with an icy slushball thrown by a playmate named Junior Barnes. So Bill makes his own snowball and stashes it in the family icebox until summertime so he can take revenge when Junior is least expecting it. Whether or not this really happened, Junior Barnes is a real person from Bill's childhood in Philadelphia, the brother of Bootsie Barnes, a close neighborhood friend.

The two albums recorded at Harrah's became hits. *Wonderfulness* went to number seven on the charts, and *Revenge* went all the way to number three. Warner Brothers followed with another Cosby album in 1968. This one was taken from sessions recorded before a live audience in Cleveland, Ohio. It was called *To Russell My Brother Whom I Slept With*. Of course, Russell actually is Bill's real-life younger brother. Bill had taken the true childhood situation of an overcrowded family and had developed it into a monologue that ran one entire side of the LP disc. Bill and Russell jump on the bed until it breaks. Then they invent excuses to their irate father, telling him that someone broke into the house and ruined the bed.

One of the last two Cosby albums issued by Warner Brothers at that time was recorded at Lake Tahoe and called *200 MPH*. The main segment is about the pleasures and perils of driving a sports car, one of Bill's favorite hobbies. The other album is called *It's True, It's True*. Cosby talks about everything from ants and shoelaces to gambling and burlesque shows. One of the longer segments is a humorous travelogue through the Far East, with stories about places Bill visited while shooting "I Spy."

Following the string of releases by Warner Brothers, Cosby produced a comedy album on his own label, Tetragrammaton. It was not particularly successful. It included two twelve-inch discs instead of one, and probably had too much loosely recorded live material to hold the listeners' interest.

Bill's next comedy albums were better received. One was entirely on sports and was called *Bill Cosby: Sports*. This was released by UNI, later called MCA. It gathers some of Bill's favorite sports stories based on his days as an athlete in high school, college, and the navy. Having excelled as an all-around athlete, Bill is able to cover a whole range of sports, from football and baseball to relays and the high jump.

In a second album put out by MCA, Cosby scored a strong hit: *Live at Madison Square Garden*. Again, part of the album is about sports. This time he talks about playing handball with a cagey old man at the YMCA. The routine is reminiscent of the handball episode on his second TV series, in which Bill demonstrates terrible sportsmanship. By the time this album was released, Bill had begun to speak not only of his own childhood but also about himself as a father. There are sections about Ennis, Erinn, and Erika. In another routine, he tells about taking his daughters to the zoo, and in one sketch, he talks about the problems that arose after the first baby was born.

This album was followed by another, on which he returns to early stories. Again released by MCA, it is called *When I Was a Kid*. Bill's brother Russell is there again, along with bits about their father, anecdotes about being in a Boy Scout troop, and stories about animals from dogs and frogs to snakes and alligators. In one of the funniest routines, Bill tells of finding out that he had a hernia in his abdomen. Every time he lifted a manhole cover, his tummy would pop out with a bump that Bill illustrates on the record with one of his many sound effects. This phenomenon makes Bill the hero of the neighborhood until the hernia is surgically repaired. The routine is an excellent example of Cosby's ability to turn a handicap into an advantage, with a lesson hidden behind the humor.

Bill's comedy production seemed endless. MCA issued two more albums full of fresh material: *For Adults Only* and *Inside the Mind of Bill Cosby*. Then Capitol Records put out two Cosby recordings. One was *My Father Confused Me, What Must I Do?* This record, issued in 1977, contained outstanding routines on parental discipline and also the now classic routine about being a victim in the dentist's chair. The other Capitol album was called *Bill's Best Friend*. The friend is a fellow named Roland Johnson who rides a roller coaster and can do tricks with his eyelids. In this album Bill touches on the drug problem with a put-down of the so-called attractions of using cocaine and marijuana. It is a subtle way of combining humor with education.

All together Bill's steady work in comedy through two decades has resulted in eighteen spoken-word albums. Several albums were released later as reissues of routines that had become classics over the years since they were first introduced. And much more recently, in 1986, an album of new club material was issued by Warners and Geffen. This is titled *Bill Cosby* and aimed primarily at parents. It contains frank but educational humor on childrearing and sex education.

No less than nine of Cosby's albums have been nominated for Grammys. Six in a row, one each year from 1964 to 1969, beginning with *I Started Out as a Child* and ending with *Bill Cosby: Sports*, won the Grammy Award for Best Comedy LP of the Year. The awards are an amazing tribute to Bill Cosby's universal humor.

After Bill Cosby's last variety show was canceled in the fall of 1976, he went through a discouraging period in which he was unwilling to get involved in another series. Steady television work was not really necessary to him, since he continued to reach audiences through club acts, recordings, TV guest appearances, and educational projects.

COSBY WRITES MUSIC

One of Bill's major interests has always been music, and he decided to pick up on this in the early 1970s by acting on several new ideas. A few years earlier he had worked on the two music albums released by Warner Brothers, *Silver Throat Sings* and *Hooray for the Salvation Army Band*. Bill had sung on these records, even though he did not have what one would call a singer's voice.

When people asked about his musical interests, Bill always said that he took up the drums at age eleven so that he could enjoy playing without having to learn to read music. And in all his years of musical activity, Bill never learned that basic skill. However, he had a good ear and an innate sense of rhythm, and he could perform well enough with skilled musicians at hand to back him up.

Because of his strength in other areas of entertainment, many people are not aware of Cosby's talents as a musician and composer. A good demonstration of this is the album he prepared for MCA with the tongue-twisting title, *Bill Cosby Presents Badfoot Brown and the Bunions Bradford Funeral and Marching Band.* After participating in the march in Atlanta, Bill had attended the funeral services for Dr. Martin Luther King, Jr. The funeral made a deep impression on Cosby, and part of this recording is an original musical reminiscence that echoed his reactions. He called it "Martin's Funeral." The entire second side of the disc is a jam session based on music composed by Cosby, which he calls "Hybish Shybish." The album was released in 1972.

The jazz recording sold quite well, and so Bill followed this two years later with another album with the same name and in the same improvisational style. This one was released by Sussex/Buddah, and again Bill wrote all of the music. Two of the pieces are sung by Stu Gardner, a musician who helped Cosby work out his musical ideas. One of the instrumentals is called "Bunions," like the record title. Some of the best music is a fascinating combination of saxophone with African-style percussion. Bill dedicated this composition to his wife, calling it "I Love You, Camille."

Cosby teamed up with Stu Gardner again in 1976, and the result was two more music albums. These were put out by Capitol, the same company that issued several of Cosby's monologue recordings. The two music discs featured rhythm-and-blues pieces, most of which were parodies of popular music. The albums were titled *Bill Cosby Is Not Himself These*

Days, Rat Own, Rat Own, Rat Own and *Disco Bill*. Cosby and Gardner worked together to write three of the songs on the albums: "Shift Down," "Happy Birthday Momma," and "One Two Three." And two songs—"Yes, Yes, Yes" and "I Luv Myself Better Than I Luv Myself"—made it as singles on the record charts.

Bill went on to produce and arrange still another Capitol music album. This one features the First Cousins Jazz Ensemble and is cleverly titled *For the Cos of Jazz*, a pun on Cosby's nickname.

Cosby has taken every chance to emphasize music and jazz during his comedy and film career, so much so that the two have become intertwined. For instance, it was comedian Allan Sherman, successful himself with song parody, who arranged for Cosby to appear on the "Tonight" show. Then later, when Bill was a guest host standing in for Johnny Carson, he brought a number of musicians onto the show, including Sonny Rollins, Max Roach, and Wynton Marsalis, a young trumpeter with a classical background who built a career as a jazz musician.

In 1986, Bill was host for a jazz and blues concert at Carnegie Hall in New York City. It was planned as part of the Kool Jazz Festival. Bill introduced such artists as B. B. King, who sang and played guitar, Arnett Cobb on saxophone, and Nat Adderley on cornet. It was a highly successful concert.

For many years Cosby has taken time to fly to Europe to attend the many jazz festivals that take place there in the summertime. At one such event in France, saxophonist James Moody and trumpeter Dizzy Gillespie were playing a lively session. Cosby,

Pianist Eubie Blake and Bill Cosby at Gallagher's restaurant in New York City, 1978.

who is a friend of both men, jumped up on the stage and began singing along in a style known as scat. Those who did not know him as a comedian accepted Cosby as simply another skilled jazz musician.

An example of Bill Cosby's willingness to help struggling musicians came in 1985 when he was scheduled for an early fall stint at the Jones Beach Theater on Long Island. As a child in Philadelphia, Bill had known the two Barnes brothers. One was the same Junior Barnes who showed up in the snowball monologue on Bill's *Revenge* album. The other was Bootsie Barnes, who loved rhythm and jazz as much as young Bill, and who later became a professional saxophone player. Bill had kept in touch with Bootsie over the years, and in 1985 he knew that Bootsie's band was playing club spots in Philadelphia for small audiences and not much money. At Cosby's invitation, the Bootsie Barnes All-Stars came to New York to open the Jones Beach event. Suddenly Bootsie was enjoying the thrill of playing a concert to a crowd of 10,000 appreciative people. Thus Bill Cosby, who had received support from so many jazz greats over the years, found an opportunity to turn around and support an old friend.

4
FAMILY MAN OF "THE COSBY SHOW"

Bill Cosby's last regular TV show had been in 1976. It was the one called "Cos," produced in Los Angeles and canceled partway into the season. Although Bill had steered clear of series TV since then, he was increasingly discouraged with much of the mediocre fare offered on television. Many serious shows seemed filled with car chases and violence, emphasizing street crime and crimes against women. The situation comedies seemed to depend too much on bizarre and far-fetched plots, quick one-line laughs, and girls looking pretty but acting ridiculous.

Some shows got laughs mainly from ethnic humor. "All in the Family" was a good example. Archie Bunker was prejudiced against blacks, Hispanics, and almost everyone who was slightly different from himself. Although Archie was ridiculously bigotted, Bill Cosby was concerned that some viewers might actually identify with Archie. Bill's position had always been to play down the differences between racial and ethnic groups, and to emphasize the human foibles they all shared. To him, this point of view seemed sadly lacking in the late seventies and early eighties.

Bill's dissatisfaction with what he saw on TV prodded him to feel that he should try to get back into series television with something different. One idea that occurred to him was to do a detective show with no violence. Instead there would be crime puzzles and solutions. All the networks rejected the idea, although sometime later a show did come along using this format with a slightly different twist. It is called "Murder, She Wrote." Looking back on this rejection of Cosby's detective suggestion, it is probably a good thing that the crime puzzler never came into being, for the idea that took its place was to become one of the most popular TV shows ever.

Bill began to think about choosing something more natural as the basis for a TV series. After all, if it was to be a show that could be watched by people of all ages, including young children, why not do a show about a family? One that would combine reality and humor.

BIRTH OF A NEW SHOW

About this time, Brandon Tartikoff, president of entertainment for NBC Television, saw Bill deliver a monologue on the "Tonight" show. It was a very effective routine about Cosby's own children. It struck Tartikoff that the material might lend itself to a new show. Two young NBC producers met with Cosby to talk about the idea. The three of them quickly agreed that a show could be developed about a family in which both parents worked. They would live in an apartment in New York City with their four children.

As the show idea evolved, several basic changes were made. At first Bill wanted to play a chauffeur, and he wanted the wife on the show to be a plumber or a carpenter. The producers argued against this, and Camille Cosby agreed with them. She told her husband that, after all, people knew he was the holder of university degrees, and they would expect his occupation to reflect that background. Camille was insistent. So Bill changed his mind and came up with the plan that the father on the show should be an obstetrician, a medical doctor who worked with women and families. Then it was decided that his wife would be a lawyer. And so a show was developed around an upper-middle-class family called the Huxtables.

As various young actors and actresses tried out for the parts of the children, it was decided that one more child could be added to the original plan. This was done to include little Keshia Knight Pulliam, who obviously would add a certain charm to the program. It also would allow Bill to do some scenes with a tiny tot, something he was especially good at. It was obvious to Bill and the producers that Keshia would need special attention and support through the long hours of preparing a show. But they all agreed it would be worth the effort. Finally, it was agreed that the TV family should have five children—four girls and one boy—like Bill's own family. In fact, when taping for the show began, the Cosbys' oldest daughter, Erika, was away at college. This suggested a parallel, and during the first few episodes the TV daughter, Sondra, was also away at college. This made the start of the series a little less complex, and offered the opportunity to introduce one of the characters later to add interest.

NBC offered to do six episodes of the series. Cosby wanted no less than thirteen guaranteed shows, and full control of the program as well. Bill also insisted that the show be produced in New York instead of Los Angeles. This was more convenient for him, but it would make the show more expensive to produce. There was one more thing Cosby demanded, which he mentioned in an interview for *Ebony* magazine: "I wanted a *huge, huge* salary."

Looking back on the advent of the show, the fact that it got under way seems miraculous. ABC had rejected the idea of a Cosby situation comedy because their marketing executives were convinced that interest in sitcoms had bottomed out. And in spite of Brandon Tartikoff's interest in Cosby's material, the comedian's demands were almost outrageous.

NBC asked for a short pilot show. For this segment Bill became "Dr. Heathcliff Huxtable" for the first time, and sat down with his TV daughters to talk about sex. NBC liked the pilot and gave the go-ahead. The network also agreed to film thirteen episodes and reluctantly arranged for the show to be shot on the East Coast. When asked about his insistence on locating in New York, Bill answered, "If I'm canceled, I'd like to be a little closer to home."

And so the logistics were worked out. Bill took an apartment in Manhattan in New York City. NBC set up a TV studio at Avenue M and Fourteenth Street in Brooklyn. It was not a Hollywood-type location. The fact that it was in an ordinary city neighborhood, though, meant that the cast and crew could walk down the street for a hot bagel and not be bothered by sightseers and autograph seekers.

CHOOSING THE CAST

The cast for the new show was almost hand-picked by Cosby himself, and the choices have proved to be excellent. Tempestt Bledsoe stood out as the best young actress to play the part of twelve-year-old Vanessa. Lisa Bonet was selected to play the somewhat older Denise. Cosby had imagined a teenager who could look a little off-balance and distracted by current fashion crazes. Lisa seemed perfect for this role. (In fact, later on, between taping for the first and second seasons of the show, she cut her hair short, something she was not supposed to do, so her new appearance had to be built into the series.) Sabrina LeBeauf was chosen for the part of Sondra, the college girl of the TV family. And tiny Keshia Knight Pulliam was written into the series as the fourth daughter, Rudy.

The hardest choice for the cast was the boy who was to play the Huxtables' only son, Theo. Several young actors seemed about equal in the auditions. Bill narrowed the selection by trying to get a more natural reaction from each boy during the audition, which consisted of a scene between father and son. The actor finally chosen was fifteen-year-old Malcolm-Jamal Warner. He tells about how it happened in his own words: "He's a perfectionist. When I first auditioned,

Cosby, as Cliff Huxtable, and Tempestt Bledsoe, as Vanessa, discuss the challenge of her placement in an advanced class at school.

Cosby, as Dr. Cliff Huxtable, and Malcolm-Jamal Warner, as his son Theo, use a Monopoly game to talk seriously about the connection between school grades and jobs on "The Cosby Show."

I played a real smart-alecky kid, huffin' and puffin'. When I finished, Mr. C. looked at me and said, 'Do you really talk to your father like that?' I said, 'No.' He said, 'Then we won't see that in the show.'" Malcolm tried the scene again, treating Cosby as he would his own father, and the realism of his acting earned him the role.

When it came to selecting the actress to play Dr. Huxtable's wife, Bill says the choice was easy. Phylicia Rashad seemed to have just the right manner. During the audition she had a way of looking the children straight in the eye as if to say that she was a mother in control who would take no nonsense. In addition, Phylicia had the natural manner of a career woman, which she would need in playing the part of a successful lawyer.

Phylicia is a graduate of Howard University with a degree in fine arts. Her father was a dentist, and her mother was a poet. Phylicia also studied theater in college. She had been a pop singer, and had serious acting experience in off-Broadway shows and with the Negro Ensemble Company. Furthermore, she was a regular on the TV series "One Life to Live." Interestingly, Phylicia's younger sister, Debbie Allen, had become well-known as the dance teacher on the series "Fame," and now Phylicia was to have her own turn at becoming a household name.

Phylicia knew that Bill Cosby felt comfortable with her after working only a short time on the series. One day in rehearsal he came up to her and said, "You have a real sense of your own space don't you? If a man came walking up to you and said, 'Sit there,' he'd be in trouble, wouldn't he?" Phylicia answered, "Yeeaahh!" Then Cosby laughed and said, "That's very good, Phylicia." Although no one could guess at the beginning, Phylicia was to become pregnant later while the series was in progress. When asked how this would change the show, she answered, "They'll shoot me from the shoulders up."

Many people ask if the private Bill Cosby is like the one they see on television. The basic answer is yes. In fact, it is the close parallel between the private Cosby and the Cosby of the TV family that makes the show so appealing. The youngsters on the show

The actors on "The Cosby Show" pose for a cast photo. From left to right, they are Tempestt Bledsoe, Malcolm-Jamal Warner, Lisa Bonet, Cosby, Phylicia Rashad, and Keshia Knight Pulliam, on Cosby's lap. Sabrina LeBeauf, who plays college-age daughter, Sondra, is not in the picture.

think of him as a father figure and sometimes come to him with their personal problems. It is not uncommon to see tiny Keshia Knight Pulliam seated on Bill's knee or next to him on the couch of the living room set, his arm around her like a father. At the same time, Bill believes in giving the cast members room

Cosby and Tempestt Bledsoe enact a scene of playful discipline with Keshia Knight Pulliam, who plays Rudy.

to create their own roles, making for natural growth within the TV family.

The respect the cast members have for Cosby extends to the crew and staff. Many black professionals have found jobs with the show. These include some of the writers and also Dr. Alvin Poussaint, a Harvard psychiatrist and special consultant to the program. The atmosphere is generally one of cooperation and mutual regard.

Director Jay Sandrich has been asked if he feels pressure to maintain the quality of the show now that it has become so popular. His answer is no, and the reason he gives is that Bill Cosby is so comfortable to work with. According to Sandrich, Cosby's manner is purposeful but relaxed so that disagreements become useful discussions rather than arguments. Sandrich feels that this natural give-and-take comes about because Bill's self-confidence allows him to let the other performers be themselves. Sandrich says, "We're not a really well-rehearsed show because of the way Bill likes to work and because we're working with children." In particular, Sandrich comments on Phylicia Rashad's contribution, explaining that she "can go along with whatever Bill's doing and at the right moment get him back on track. She's not a comedienne; she's something at least as rare: an actress who can do comedy."

However, in spite of the informal atmosphere, according to contract, Cosby has full control over the TV series. Sandrich chuckles as he explains that sometimes when he is trying to persuade Cosby to do a scene his way, Bill will nod, apparently in agreement. Then without saying anything to Sandrich, Cosby will go off and do it his own way anyhow. Of course, if it works, who can argue with the outcome?

About the time the show got under way, the press was naturally interested in whether the latest Cosby effort could be a success. Reporters also were curious about how Bill felt after being away from series TV for so many years. Cosby has always understood the importance of good publicity, and certainly it was important at that time. However, like many other entertainers, he has often been disappointed by interviews in which he expressed his views clearly, only to have reporters publish their own thoughts instead of Cosby's actual statements. As a result, when magazines wanted to do articles on Cosby, he turned them down unless they agreed to put his picture on the cover. Some magazines responded to this demand in the interest of attracting readers. Others, such as *People* magazine, refused to conform. Apparently the cover guarantee had to be presented to Cosby in a formal letter from the magazine, and this was something *People* would not do because it limited the magazine's editorial choice.

Sometimes Cosby gives interviews in which his answers are tape-recorded and quoted word for word, making for accurate reporting. However, he can be uncooperative to writers seeking information if he does not agree with the thrust of their particular projects. Thus Bill Cosby has come to have a dual reputation in the eyes of the press. On the one hand, he is seen as a congenial and open person, genuinely friendly and helpful. On the other hand, he is sometimes perceived as a person who is defensive, aloof, and even arrogant. The views seem to conflict until one realizes that Bill Cosby is a complex man with his own strengths and shortcomings. The fact that the positive image well outweighs the negative one is a credit to the choices Cosby has made in both his personal and his public life.

Whatever the press and the critics thought about the new Cosby venture, the success of the fresh series surprised almost everyone. In its first season, the show quickly surged to number one in the ratings, outdistancing such popular shows as "Magnum, P.I.," which was then opposite it in the same time slot. "The Cosby Show" remained in first place against almost all competition, even specials like the Academy Awards ceremony. Viewership for the summer reruns was outstanding. There was no question that the series would be renewed for a second season.

By April 1986, NBC finally moved ahead of CBS in the TV ratings war. Most of the credit goes to "The Cosby Show," along with another family comedy, "Family Ties"; "Golden Girls," a sitcom about senior citizens; and the police show "Miami Vice." Cosby once told *Ebony* magazine, "I'm going to take this show and make it last as long as I can to show black people that they have something to be proud of." Cosby certainly has made good his intentions. The fact that his show crosses racial barriers with its common family theme has brought a huge audience from all segments of the American population, and a broad age range from youngsters to senior citizens.

CELEBRITY SHOWCASE
"The Cosby Show" has become a spotlight for many well-known entertainers who appear from time to time on episodes of the series. The scripts are so well written that the appearances of these celebrities seem totally natural. They all seem to be a part of the flow of the show rather than something plugged in just to attract viewers.

A number of these famous guests are musicians, and some are introduced in surprising ways. For example, one episode features music by Ray Charles and the Raelettes. The musicians do not appear on camera. Rather, a recording of their music is used for a pantomime in which the whole Huxtable family dances and lip-syncs the lyrics. The family members use the stairs as a stage, and everyone has a turn for a solo with appropriate dance steps thrown in. Little Rudy steals the show by taking the part of Ray Charles himself.

In another episode, Denise and Theo are out driving the family car. They come home to tell their parents about being in an accident. The two teenagers seem strangely overjoyed about this. The reason, it turns out, is that a limousine ran into them at a slippery intersection. And in the limousine was none other than rock singer Stevie Wonder. Wonder apologizes and invites all the Huxtables to one of his taping sessions.

At the studio Stevie is using a synthesizer that has a digital sound-recording memory. He manages to capture bits of random sound from the Huxtables almost without their knowing it, and he surprises them by playing back the segments, which repeat like echoes. The sounds come out at the pitch of any note he plays on the keyboard. For instance, Dr. Huxtable's voice emerges sounding as if he is singing "Baby, Baby, Baby," in a deep base voice.

Stevie surprises Clair by asking her to sing along with him. Phylicia, who plays Clair, actually has had experience as a professional singer, and the episode with Stevie Wonder takes advantage of this. It is a hilarious but very musical jam session combining Stevie, Clair, and the prerecorded Huxtable family sounds, all of it good enough to hit the pop charts.

Another episode has special guest scenes with singer Lena Horne, a favorite of Bill Cosby. On the

In this episode of "The Cosby Show" the Huxtable family is invited backstage to visit with singer Lena Horne after her performance.

show, the Huxtable family hears Lena in a club act and has a chance to visit with her backstage.

In still another episode, singer Joe Williams plays Clair's father, who is visiting the Huxtables. Williams is a fine actor and very convincing in his role. In one scene he is sitting with Clair on the living room couch. The two of them are remembering good times, and they wind up singing a spontaneous but beautiful duet. The musical fragment has a perfectly natural place in the flow of the dialogue.

Joe Williams also sings in a memorable episode during the following season. In one segment, Theo learns about the history of racial protest firsthand from his parents and grandparents, who were in the famous

Memphis March. Williams quietly sings the "Battle Hymn of the Republic." His voice is both a part of the TV story and an echo of history.

Other Cosby interests can be noticed in various touches on the stage sets for the TV show. Of course, the home interior and furnishings are those of a well-to-do upper-middle-class family, since Cliff Huxtable is a doctor and Clair is a lawyer. An addition to the sets is a selection of paintings by black artist Varnette Honeywood. These are grouped on the walls in various parts of the house. Honeywood is one of Cosby's favorite artists, and the paintings are excellent as well as appropriate. Another unique item is visible on the wall in Theo's bedroom. It is an anti-apartheid poster protesting racial prejudice in South Africa. The sign is there only because Bill insisted on it over the objections of NBC executives. And on the door in Denise's bedroom hangs a picture of the late Martin Luther King, Jr. Although the viewing audience is not consciously aware of most of these background details, they help to set the tone of the show as being serious behind the humor.

It was natural that the children who play the Huxtable youngsters on TV would become acquainted with the real Cosby children. When Malcolm-Jamal Warner first met Ennis, the two tried playing basketball together at the Cosby farmhouse. Ennis was six feet four, and Malcolm was only five feet six, so this was a lop-sided mismatch. But the two share common interests and have become firm friends. In fact both boys call Bill "Dad." Though a few years older than her TV counterpart, Bill's youngest daughter, Evin, and Keshia

Bill Cosby running a relay lap in a competition for the forty-and-over age group in 1983.

Knight Pulliam also have become close. Bill says they often gang up on him and kid him about his "tummy." Cosby is a bit sensitive about this tendency to a slight middle-age bulge and complains that he doesn't have enough time to run it off by jogging.

He did, however, run in the Penn Relay competition in the forty-and-over age group in 1983. Just to illustrate how closely the TV show resembles real life, Dr. Huxtable also ran in a relay race. In this episode, Cosby is overly confident of his victory, when unbeknownst to him, his opponent becomes ill and is

Camille Cosby enjoys the races flanked by her husband and Valerie
Briscoe Hooks, the Olympic runner who embarrasses Dr. Huxtable by
passing him in the relay segment shot for the show.

replaced at the last minute by the formidable Olympic
runner, Valerie Briscoe Hooks. Valerie easily over-
takes the startled Dr. Huxtable while he is waving to
the spectators in the stands.

Twenty-five episodes of "The Cosby Show" are
written for each TV season, and all of them are taped
in the Brooklyn studio. Actually each completed tape
is made of takes from two separate runs, one shot on
Thursday afternoon at 4:30, and the other shot on
Thursday evening at 8:30. What the audience sees
later on TV is a combination of the best clips from
the two shooting sessions.

A studio audience watches each taping to supply
the response and laughter. The audience may be

warmed up by a comic or may see some tapes of earlier shows. Members of the audience are sometimes given the opportunity to ask questions of the producer, Caryn Sneider, or a writer, or occasionally Cosby himself. By the time taping begins, the audience is already into the spirit of the new episode. No applause signs are needed.

Four separate sets occupy the stage. To the left is the master bedroom. Next to it is the kitchen. Adjacent to this is the living room, and almost offstage to the right are the upstairs hall and the children's bedrooms. TV cameras, crew, and actors move in and out of these stage rooms shooting brief scenes. During the breaks, the cast and crew change camera angles and locations.

The atmosphere is informal but businesslike. On the one hand, Cosby might kid around between takes to keep people relaxed. On the other hand, he might make a terse comment to keep the others in line. There are hurried conferences among staff members. Most noticeable is a natural give-and-take, with each actor helping to develop the mood. Four TV cameras are busy shooting the scenes from many angles at the same time, any one of which may be selected later during the editing process. If things go well on Thursday, it is because of the hard work that has been put in at rehearsals earlier in the week, where lines are memorized and problems are ironed out with the script, props, or actions.

During its first season, "The Cosby Show" received eight Emmy nominations. Bill refused the nomination for Best Actor in a Comedy Series, feeling that he had received more than his share of awards in the past. In its second season Cosby turned down the nomination once again, but the show won three other Emmy awards. About the success of his show, Bill has said, "I didn't do it so people could vote on whether Bill Cosby is better than so and so. . . . I don't want my fellow actors to feel they are competing with me."

Holding the number one spot in the TV ratings has made "The Cosby Show" an outstanding financial success for NBC. As the popularity of the show increased, the fees that could be charged for advertising time rose dramatically. In its second year the series brought in nearly $93 million, almost double the revenue from the first year. And NBC raised the price for only *one second* of advertising to $400,000—the highest rate in the history of TV!

Because of the competition, some of the series airing opposite "The Cosby Show" moved to time slots on other nights for the 1986 season. However, "The Cosby Show" continues to air on Thursday night. Millions of viewers tune in faithfully at 8:00 P.M. to watch a half-hour of enjoyable family comedy. Even the show opener is appealing. Bill Cosby worked with arranger Stu Gardner to develop the theme music, titled "Rasta Farsan." Thanks to their inventive collaboration, the theme is as up-to-date and funky as any on television.

The musical beat begins, set up by a bass line that Cosby helped to improvise at one of the recording sessions. The entire Huxtable clan comes on and off camera to ham it up with brief dance routines laid over the theme. The older children and Mrs. Huxtable all do tidbits, ending with tiny Rudy bouncing up and down while pumping her arms. Finally Cosby is left alone doing an overcontrolled and awkward step of his own in which he looks laughably unable to move. According to Bill, in order to introduce variety, a new way of introducing the shows is planned for the fall 1987 series. But whatever the opener, it sets the mood. And once again the foibles, antics, love, and humor of America's favorite TV family are watched by viewers who know ahead of time that they are not going to be disappointed.

BILL COSBY, THE AUTHOR

At the height of Cosby's TV popularity, in the spring of 1986, a project came to completion that had been in preparation for some time. Doubleday published a book written by Bill Cosby. It is called *Fatherhood*. Cosby often had been approached about writing his autobiography, but he had always turned down the idea. Much had already been written about him. Through his films, TV shows, record albums, and interviews, Bill had been almost continuously in the public eye. And most people were aware that some of the material on the new TV show reflected events in Bill's own family.

Bill is also a very private person, uninterested in passing out information or making himself vulnerable to the public. This wall of privacy extends to his family. Indeed this may be one important reason that he has been successful as a family man and as an entertainer at the same time. But although Bill had rejected the idea of writing a straight autobiography, he was

97

The Cosby children, Ensa, 7, Ennis, 12, Erinn, 13, and Erika, 15, surround their mother after she received a degree from the University of Massachusetts, Amherst, 1981.

extremely interested in education and childrearing. So, when someone suggested that he write a book about raising children and facing the problems of family life, he agreed to do so. The result was *Fatherhood*.

The volume has a foreword and an afterword by Alvin Poussaint, the professor of psychiatry who also is a consultant to the show. The book itself is a collection of short chapters on everything from natural childbirth to teenage traumas and the problems of sending youngsters to college. The chapters are really Bill Cosby's reminiscences of his own experiences over the years. He avoids calling his children by name in his anecdotes, but the reader often can guess which one he is referring to. Some of the incidents are true. Many are exaggerated in Bill's typical style, and a few sound like his comedy monologues or scenes right out of the new TV show.

The anecdotes are humorous stories with built-in lessons and pointers from a father of five who speaks from his own experience. Although Bill's wife, Camille, was a college major in child psychology and Bill himself had a minor in child psychology at Temple, he does not pretend to speak as an expert. With tongue in cheek he writes that "some people have several children because they know there are going to be failures. They figure if they have a dozen, maybe one or two will work out, for having children is certainly defying the odds." Bill even claims that his own father once said, "I brought you into this world and I can take you out. It don't make no difference to me. I'll just make another one like you."

Bill admits that discipline is one of the most difficult things for a parent to learn. As an aid, he humorously suggests that parents give each child a name that ends with a vowel so that the sound will carry when they have to shout at the child out the window.

Bill believes that physical punishment should be used very sparingly. One chapter is titled "Speak Loudly and Carry a Small Stick," a turn-around of the famous statement once made by President Theodore Roosevelt, "Speak softly and carry a big stick." Bill obviously believes that children can learn best through example. But there are exceptions. He remembers that his mother used to threaten to "take a stick and knock your brains out!" Bill also recalls his response: "All during my stormy boyhood years, I wanted to get some calves' brains and keep them in my pocket. Then, when my mother hit me on the head, I would throw them on the floor. Knowing her, however, she merely would have said, 'Put your brains back in your head! Don't *ever* let your brains fall out of your head! Have you lost your *mind*?"

He writes of an incident with his own son, whom he had always been reluctant to strike. But according to Bill, at age twelve the lad developed a habit of evading the truth to cover up low grades and other problems at school. Finally, Bill took the boy out to the barn and spanked him. The result was that Bill and Camille received a letter from the school about how well their son was doing. Obviously in this instance the exception proved the rule. Much later on "Donahue," Cosby was questioned about this same incident. He responded, "I did not hit this boy when I was angered and wanted to kill." Bill's philosophy was that the physical punishment was a fulfillment of his promise of disciplinary action.

Bill also writes of the failures of contemporary education. He cannot understand why his own children, born in an English-speaking country, should get poor grades in English, and he constantly admonishes them to learn proper use of their native tongue. Cosby is critical of the swing away from basic classroom skills and the lack of substance in school curricula. He says that when he attended college, he occasionally cut classes and went to the movies but that today the movies themselves have become the class, or as it is commonly termed, the "film experience." Bill writes, "I just feel that for eighty thousand dollars a student should spend four years in a school where English comes up from time to time. I cannot stand to see it being scaled *down* to the students. The students should be reaching up to *it* because success in life demands the use of intellect under pressure."

There is a chapter on music and the rift between the generations. Bill says that when he was thirteen, his father used to listen to music by Duke Ellington and Count Basie. Disdaining these choices, Bill would sneak upstairs to listen to Sonny Rollins, Dizzy Gillespie, Miles Davis, and Thelonious Monk. Of course, he listened at top volume, and just as Bill was to do later with his own youngsters, his father would march in and shout, "Turn that crap down!" Bill goes on to complain that today's teenage music is sheer nonsense with dirty lyrics. He surmises that the only reason children choose certain music is because they know their parents hate it.

One of Bill Cosby's favorite topics is independence. After parents spend a fortune sending their offspring through college, the least the children can do, he feels, is not to continue to sponge off the family. Bill makes this point strongly in his book, and he echoed it during a special event in which he participated after the book was finished.

In the spring of 1986, Bill Cosby—Dr. William Cosby to the academic community—was asked to give the commencement address at the University of South Carolina. He challenged the graduating students to accept full responsibility for their lives and careers. And part of this responsibility, he said, was to learn to live independently. Cosby told the graduates that all across the nation at commencement addresses, speakers were telling students to "go forth." And, admonished Cosby with one of his favorite lines, " 'forth' is not back home."

Cosby's book was published a few weeks before Father's Day. It was very good timing for a book whose title was *Fatherhood*, and sales immediately soared making the book into a bestseller. Between the success of the book and the impact of the TV series, Cosby became the ideal person to interview. He was seen often on "Entertainment Tonight," "PM Magazine," and various talk shows. In one interview Bill was asked about divorced parents. He quipped that when one parent has custody of the children, the other decides to try to get them back, believing that the first parent is doing everything wrong. And so the kids bounce back and forth, with each parent trying his or her luck for a time. Cosby joked that married parents have no such options. They have to keep the children: "There's no place to send them."

When asked about the writing of his book, Cosby admits that Camille asked him to take certain things out, and Bill honored her feelings by removing them. The result is a book that is personal but at the same time keeps a certain distance, as if not to give away too many family secrets. One interviewer asked Cosby if his youngsters had read the book before it was published. He answered no, saying, "They'll write *their* books later!"

It is obvious that Cosby's elevation to America's number one father figure exerts pressure on him to live up to his reputation. According to Bill, this is not a strain. Nevertheless, he admits "I've got about a hundred million people monitoring me." The statement is not far from the truth. But the judgment is overwhelmingly positive. In 1986, he won the People's Choice Award for Favorite All Around Male Entertainer. And at the finish of the 1986 season, "The Cosby Show" remained a strong first in the TV ratings. Bill's comments and opinions are in demand everywhere. And he has capitalized on his popularity by lending his name as a spokesperson for important benefits and charities.

For example, in July 1985, Bill appeared at a concert at Robin Hood Dell East in Philadelphia. There he introduced a benefit for the residents of Osage Avenue, whose homes had been destroyed in a fire in West Philadelphia. Later, during the spring of 1986, Cosby was designated—along with singer Kenny Rogers and baseball star Pete Rose—as one of three planners for Hands Across America. This was an offshoot of the earlier Live Aid benefit for African relief, which had been so successful worldwide. Hands Across America was an attempt to call attention to the plight of poor Americans by designating May 27 as the day for people to join hands and form a human chain stretching from the West Coast to the East Coast. Thanks to the support and endorsement of Cosby and other celebrities, including President Reagan, the effort was essentially successful.

Just as he helped musician Bootsie Barnes by in-

Bill Cosby and the American Boychoir School provided entertainment
for a benefit concert in New Jersey. Here New Jersey Governor
Thomas Kean helps display the sweatshirt Cosby accepted designating
him an honorary member of the choir.

viting him to a Long Island benefit concert, Cosby
continued to assist people he had been close to in the
past. One old friend bought a McDonald's franchise
in Reno, Nevada. Bill graciously appeared at the open-
ing, attracting thousands of people by signing photo-
graphs, record albums, windbreakers, sneakers, plastic
footballs, and even paper napkins. One little girl in
the crowd was awestruck at seeing Cosby, who was

wearing a red jogging outfit. She whispered to her mother, "Is that Santa Claus?" Her mother answered, "No dear, that's Bill Cosby. He's *better* than Santa Claus."

Sometimes Bill just likes to touch base with places he has known in the past. One of these is in Washington, D.C. When Bill was courting Camille, he used to travel from New York City to the Washington area to spend time with her. One of their favorite diversions was to stop at a place called Ben's Chili, where they could get frankfurters, sausages, and chili with lots of onions. Bill used to kid Camille about having onions on her breath. In spite of that old joke, Bill has gone back to Ben's Chili for a nostalgic visit almost every year for at least twenty years.

Travel around the country is made easier by the fact that Bill now owns a seven-passenger Mitsubishi jet airplane, ready to go almost anywhere at a moment's notice. And of course the Cosbys can easily afford more than one home. Today they have four residences. There is the family farmhouse in Amherst, Massachusetts. They also own a Manhattan town house, located conveniently close to the Brooklyn studio where the show is taped. They have a third place in Los Angeles, where Camille spends time working as a producer on projects such as Bill's latest comedy albums.

Recently, the Cosbys remodeled a Victorian house in Cheltenham, north of Philadelphia. It was chosen to provide a residence close to the George School, a Philadelphia area high school now attended by two of the Cosby youngsters. It probably is no accident that the Cheltenham home is very close to Germantown, where Bill grew up, and not far from Temple University, where he started college and where he now is a member of the board of trustees. It is certainly a location that connects the Cosby past to the Cosby present.

Even in the Cheltenham home, Bill's educational philosophy is evident. The large house has three floors, and the upper story holds the teenagers' bedrooms. When showing the house to guests, Bill points out with pride that the third floor has no TV sets. The space is for sleeping and studying only.

It is his attention to his family, his friends, his past, and his deepest roots that keeps Bill Cosby a stable and caring person in the midst of a career that easily could become too much to handle.

He remains secure in himself and his workable philosophy of life, giving credit where it is due. Of his wife he says, "My life now is a very happy one. It's a happiness of being deeply connected, of knowing there is someone I can trust completely, and that the one I trust is the one I love. With her strength and help, I can only become better, and I want to because I want her to be proud of me."

And Bill remains devoted to his children, some of whom are now grown up and ready to "go forth," as he would put it. Perhaps his advice on how to be a successful person and parent at the same time is best summed up at the end of one chapter of his book, *Fatherhood*:

*And here's the whole challenge of being a parent.
Even though your kids will constantly do the exact
opposite of what you tell them to do, you have to keep
loving them just as much. To any question about your
response to a child's strange behavior, there is really
just one answer: give them love. I make a lot of money
and I've given a lot to charities, but I've given all of
myself to my wife and kids, and that's the best do-
nation I'll ever make.*

This is the Bill Cosby we all know best.

ACKNOWLEDGEMENTS

The author wishes to thank the following people for contributing information, materials, or helpful suggestions:

Gavin White, Jr., associate professor of physical education, and former director of athletics and head track coach, Temple University, Philadelphia

Doris White, Wildwood Crest, NJ

George Brightbill, curator, photojournalism collection, Temple University, Philadelphia

Zohrab Kazanjian, photographer, Audio-Visual Department, Temple University, Philadelphia

Charles Blockson, curator, Afro-American collection, Philadelphia

George Ingram, director, Temple University News Bureau, Philadelphia

Robert Brothers, assistant editor, *Temple Times*, Philadelphia

Al Shrier, director of sports information, assistant director of athletics, Temple University, Philadelphia

Ed Mahan, photographer, Philadelphia

Dave Coskey, photographer, Clementon, NJ

Linda Seidman, Archives, University Library, University of Massachusetts at Amherst

Herb Hartnett, director of sports information, University of Pennsylvania, Philadelphia

Ellen Rodman, vice president corporate communications, Children's Television Workshop, New York City

PHOTO CREDITS

A NOTE ON SOURCES

The author drew upon the following sources for certain factual information and incidental quotes:

ARTICLES

"Cosby!" Brad Darrach, *Life*, June 1985.

"The Cosby Show," Lynn Norment, *Ebony*, April 1985.

"The Evolution of a Comic Named Cosby," James McBride, *Philadelphia Enquirer*, November 17, 1985.

"A Father's Day Tribute: Bill Cosby Talks about Raising Children," Stephanie Stokes Oliver, *Essence*, June 1984.

"Playboy Interview: Bill Cosby," Lawrence Linderman, *Playboy*, December 1985.

"Please, Mr. Cosby, Build on Your Own Success," Mary Helen Washington, *TV Guide*, March 22, 1986.

"She'll Show You the Serenity—But Not the Strife,"
Roderick Townley, *TV Guide*, September 7, 1985.

BOOKS

Bill Cosby—For Real, Caroline Latham, TOR Books,
1985.
Bill Cosby: Look Back in Laughter, James T. Olson, Cre-
ative Education, 1977.
Bill Cosby: Making America Laugh and Learn, Harold
and Geraldine Woods, Dillon Press, 1983.
Cosby, Ronald L. Smith, St. Martin's, 1986.
Education's Smoking Guns, Reginald G. Damerell,
Freundlich, 1985.
Fatherhood, Bill Cosby, Doubleday, 1986.
You Are Somebody Special, Charles Shedd, Quest, 1978.

TELEVISION INTERVIEWS

"CBS Morning News," CBS Television
"Entertainment Tonight," ABC Television
"Live at Five," NBC Television
"PM Magazine," Fox Television
"Donahue," NBC Television

INDEX

ABOUT THE AUTHOR

Larry Kettelkamp received a BFA degee in painting from the University of Illinois, and studied illustration at the Pratt Institute, Brooklyn, New York. He has worked as a staff artist for the magazine *Highlights for Children*. Also a musician and composer, he has worked as editor of Summy Birchard music publisher. Kettelkamp is a frequent workshop lecturer on creativity and the preparation of text and illustration for junior books. Currently he teaches Graphic Design at Rider College in New Jersey, and directs Bookarts Associates, his own publication, design, and production service.

Larry Kettelkamp is the author/illustrator of more than thirty-five books for children and young adults, including those on sports, music, technology, and the life and health sciences.